# Pathways
## to
# Peace

*Lessons to Inspire Peace in the
Early Childhood Classroom*

## KIMBERLY PAQUETTE

iUniverse, Inc.
New York   Bloomington

Pathways to Peace
Lessons to Inspire Peace in the Early Childhood Classroom

iUniverse books may be ordered through booksellers or by contacting:

iUniverse
1663 Liberty Drive
Bloomington, IN 47403
www.iuniverse.com
1-800-Authors (1-800-288-4677)

ISBN: 978-1-4401-6131-5 (pbk)
ISBN: 978-1-4401-6132-2 (ebk)

Printed in the United States of America

iUniverse rev. date: 8/18/2009

I dedicate this curriculum to those committed to providing our children with the tools necessary to construct and build a peaceful tomorrow. The world is waiting for these young peacemakers to arrive, and I commend and applaud all those who will help them along the way.

# Contents

# Preface

Montessori teacher training is intense. It can be exhilarating, inspiring, and grueling all at the same time. I remember sitting in a beautiful classroom at Walnut Park Montessori School in Newton, Massachusetts, where I began my Montessori education. Every day, for two summers in a row, I would make the commute into Newton to learn about the philosophy, methods, materials, and visions of Montessori. I was struck by how concrete the lessons seemed to be. What a gift for children to be given the opportunity to learn any given subject employing all of their senses. It seemed so simple, yet also complex. I instantly fell in love and knew I was at home.

During my coursework and internship, my own children were great teachers to me. I practiced giving lessons to them and sought their opinions when developing new materials. They were eager learners but did not hold back in giving feedback as to how to improve not only myself, but the materials I was preparing for the classroom. Education really became a family endeavor.

I spent several years as a classroom teacher, working with the children in math, language, cultural studies, etc. I visited other schools to see how they were doing things. I attended conferences and workshops from one side of the country to the other. I was eager to learn more and improve my contributions to the classroom. It was interesting to me to find that many schools had set up areas of their classrooms for peaceful reflection. Some had books or aquariums set up in a corner of the classroom; others had labyrinths and Zen gardens; and others still had pictures, inspirational quotes, and cozy pillows. Then there were schools that did not have so-called peace corners, yet exuded peace in their actions and messages. I began to wonder ….

My wondering landed me right in graduate school, working on a peace education curriculum for teachers to use as a guide. Our training prepared us quite well in the core academic areas, yet those out in the field seemed to be left to their own devices when it came to the peaceful education of our children. Feeling that this was too important a subject to leave to interpretation, I dove into this work headfirst and took my family with me again. It took two years, but together we came up with a curriculum that was rooted in the concrete, was both simple and complex, and received two thumbs up from my children.

This curriculum allows teachers to include peace in all aspects of their classrooms. It doesn't have to be something relegated to isolated corners of the class or reserved for special occasions. Peace is all around us, and it only makes sense for our children to see it as ever present and a part of life. This is my work. This is our work. Together, we can support the peaceful education of our kids. It is intense. It can be exhilarating, inspiring, and grueling all at the same time. And it is worth every second.

# Acknowledgments

This project would not have come to fruition without the help and support of many dedicated people who selflessly gave their time, energy, and expertise. I would like to thank Marion Nesbit, who was able to help me see the steps necessary to get to the end. Thanks to Mary Gale, whose knowledge and experience has inspired me to pursue the call to become a Montessori leader, and to Erin Gutierrez for her ability to empathize and visualize what this project could become. Thank you all for being a wonderfully dedicated team, without whom, I fear, I would not have been able to produce this work.

I owe many thanks to Bonnie LaMothe and the instructors at NEMTEC for providing me with the building blocks and training to become a well-equipped Montessori teacher. Thank you also to the Montessorians and educators alike who have inspired me to keep peace education at the forefront of my mind: Sonnie McFarland, Aline Wolfe, and Rosemary Clough.

Thank you to Connie Mercier, who saw my potential and gave me the support and encouragement I needed to become a Montessori teacher. You have been a wonderful director, a loving friend, and an amazing mentor. Thanks also to the children and families at the Auburn Children's House in Auburn, New Hampshire. I have learned so much from my time with you and have enjoyed being part of such a supportive community.

Thank you to my gracious and supporting husband, who held my hand and encouraged me to continue at every turn. Israel, thank you for hearing the things I never had to say and for saying the things I needed to hear.

Finally, I need to thank two of the most amazing budding peacemakers I know, my daughters, Haelie Jane and Abby Rose. Haelie, thank you for offering your bedroom when your mom needed a quiet space to write, and thank you for continuing to make me proud as you spread peace through your art and message. Abby, thank you for volunteering to demonstrate yoga poses or peaceful work to the younger children in your life and for allowing me to test every lesson and work on you. I could not have finished this without the inspiration and motivation you two girls have provided. Thank you!

# Introduction

This work provides a peace curriculum intended for the Montessori three- to six-year-old classroom, though it may be used in other early childhood settings. Although Maria Montessori had much to say on the topic of peace education, little has been published in the way of lessons for the teacher to incorporate into the classroom. This curriculum combines Maria Montessori's educational method and Howard Gardner's Theory of Multiple Intelligences to provide a curriculum aimed at reaching teachers, educators, and care providers of young children. The format of the lessons, while rooted in the Montessori approach, can and should be adapted to fit other programs. The purpose of this peace education curriculum is to provide children with exposure to peaceful symbols, practices, and language.

What is peace? Is it merely the absence of war? The primary aim of war in history has been the acquisition of land and conquest of its people. In the aftermath of war, the loss, the devastation, and the helplessness, the abolishment of races and the destruction of culture are all too often the effects … is that how peace shall be defined? Of the various definitions of the word, peace can be defined as "the normal, non-warring condition of a nation, group of nations, or the world" (www. dictionary. com). Even when nations are not in a state of war, however, peace cannot be guaranteed."The fact that we mistakenly call the permanent triumph of the aims of war 'peace' causes us to fail to recognize the way to salvation, the path that could lead us to true peace" (Montessori, 1949, p. 6).

In the field of peace education, the primary objective is not to find a way to end war or to bring warring nations together. The aim of peace education is to allow peace to manifest itself in the hearts of the children we serve. The children are the future of our society, our nations, and our planet. The children are our salvation, and it is the mission of peace educators to show them the path that could lead us all toward true peace. The education of children is the best weapon for peace.

Children are being raised within a complex society with its own set of problems and obstacles. It is known that children in our country are treading in the midst of violence stemming from multiple sources: domestic violence, violence within their communities, violence in the news and media, and violence modeled in their play and games (Levin and Carlson-Paige, 1998, p. 31). More often, children are being presented with their own sets of challenges, often times without having the tools to handle them."From the Arctic to the Equator, from South America to Southeast Asia, children all around the world are busy doing the same things ... they worry about wars and wish for peace" (Copsey, 1995, p. 1). The desire for peace is universal.

Peace education can provide children with the tools necessary to deal with change and adversity throughout their lives. In today's fast-paced, technology-rich world, it can be tempting to join the race and work to an end result at breakneck speeds. However, without slowing down and showing children what the world has to offer, children will not know the beauty the world holds, that which is worth protecting, nor will they be inclined to see the beauty and spirit of those around them (Sherlock, 2003, p. 4). Peace education can be a lesson in the art of simplicity. It can also be a lesson in turning inward to find calm in the midst of chaos. Peace education, when presented in a well thought-out manner, can inspire children to be the future peacemakers of our world and ultimately lead this future generation toward the development of a peaceful planet.

Several programs and approaches are thought to be connected to the application of peace education in early childhood education. Some examples include: Montessori education, the work of the United Nations, self-esteem building, cooperative learning, and conflict resolution (Montessori, 1949; Cunningham, 2008; Reasoner, 2008; Johnson, Johnson, and Holubec, 1990; Wheeler, Stomfay-Stitz, 2006). This work briefly reviews these peace education programs and approaches. It is hypothesized that by combining the essence of Montessori education with these approaches and the current research supporting the theories of Multiples Intelligences and Social-Emotional Learning, a more inclusive and complete curriculum for peace education may be derived (Gardner, 2006; Goleman, 1995; Elias, 2004).

# Part One:
# Academic Underpinnings and Context

# A Brief Review of Peace Education Programs and Approaches

The following review represents a concise synopsis of the presence of peace education throughout history. Peace education is not something new. It has been recognized throughout past centuries, albeit with several various names, labels, and guises. Peace is first mentioned in some of the earliest writings we have access to. In fact, aspects of peace education can be traced through many, if not most, of the texts written and used by the major world religions. Passages like "The whole of the Torah is for the purpose of promoting peace," as read in the Talmud, or "Blessed are the peacemakers, for they shall be called sons of God," as read in the Bible, or the Buddhist scripture Digha Nikaya, "He brings together those who are divided, he encourages those who are friendly; he is a peacemaker, a lover of peace, impassioned for peace, a speaker of words that make for peace." Religious choices aside, these early writings all reflect peaceful sentiments and the desire for a peaceful world (http://www. unification. net/ws/theme074. htm).

People have been working for and promoting peace since the beginning of history, from Martin Luther King Jr. to Mahatma Ghandi and from Albert Einstein to the Dalai Lama, to name a few. There have been pioneers who have tried to find the best ways of establishing peace. Throughout history, many thinkers have agreed that the most effective and promising way to promote peace in the world is to begin with the child. Although the work has been done by educators like Maria Montessori, Sonnie McFarland, and Ursula Thrush; theorists including Howard Gardner and Daniel Goleman; psychologists William James and Jean Piaget; social activists, including Mahatma Ghandi and Jane Goodall; and others, the basic tenet remains the same. There is tremendous value in teaching and raising our children, our youngest citizens, to be peaceful.

The following represents a brief review of a few selected curricular approaches to peace education. This review includes an early approach to peace education designed by an Italian scientist and proposed candidate for the Nobel Peace Prize, Dr. Maria Montessori (1949). International organizations are represented in their quest for furthering peace education for children (UN Resolutions A/RES/52/13 : *Culture of Peace* and A/RES/53/243, *Declaration and Programme of*

*Action on a Culture of Peace*, Elias, 2004). The following sections on Maria Montessori, the work of the United Nations, self-esteem building, cooperative learning and conflict resolution, provide a rationale and implications for peace education.

## MARIA MONTESSORI

In 1896, Maria Montessori became the first woman in Italy to become a medical doctor (Standing, 1957, p. 27). In her work as a doctor with children housed in insane asylums, she felt a longing, and surely a call, to help them. It was through the observations of these children and her work with them that Montessori became aware that "mental deficiency was a pedagogical problem rather than a medical one" (Standing, 1957, p. 28). Through years of observation and an uncanny sense of child development and potential, Montessori designed an educational pedagogy serving the fundamental needs of children. Her theory spoke to the natural developmental periods of all children and provided an education for academic, social, emotional, physical, and spiritual learning.

Maria Montessori saw the potential in each child to bring the world closer to the attainment of peace. She was concerned by the trends she observed in education. In her observations, she failed to see children being taught to help each other and work together, but conversely, to concern themselves with getting their own high marks and being promoted each year. Their interaction with classmates was in a competitive manner as opposed to a cooperative team-building approach. The system seemed to create selfish, tired children, isolated from each other.

"And these poor, selfish little creatures, who experimental psychology has proved are mentally exhausted, find themselves in later life separate grains of sand in the desert, each one is isolated from his neighbor, and all of them are barren. If a storm comes up, these little human particles possessed of no life-giving spirituality are caught up in the gusts and form a deadly whirlwind. An education capable of saving humanity is no small undertaking; it involves the spiritual development of man, the enhancement of his value as an individual, and the preparation of young people to understand the times in which they live" (Montessori, 1949, p. 35).

Maria Montessori created an educational pedagogy which extended well beyond the academic goals placed before children in typical classroom settings. Her pedagogy included a deep respect for children and the spiritual development of their psyche. Her aims included assisting in the development of the whole child and preparing them for society, life, and the quest for inner peace. Receiving high marks in mathematics had its value, but it seemed insignificant if a child would grow up unaware of how to peacefully react to or work together with others. With that in mind, Montessori concluded that preparing children for life was in the best interest of society. She felt it was necessary to address these social concerns through the education of children (Montessori, 1949, p. 56).

Montessori recognized the spiritual side of children and realized that it was the work of parents and educators to nurture and protect that spirit. She traveled the globe giving speeches and writing papers reflecting the importance and significance of peace and education. A series of speeches and addresses given by Montessori were combined and published in her book entitled *Education and Peace* in 1949. Although written more than a half century ago, the messages and concerns found therein could have been written today."Education today is still confined by the limits of a social order that is now past ... an extremely important social task lies before us: actuating man's value, allowing him to attain the maximum development of his energies, truly preparing him to bring about a different form of human society on a higher plane" (Montessori, 1949, p. xi). Montessori contended that through the spiritual development of the child, children would be better prepared to contribute to society and work peacefully as individuals and cooperatively with others (1949). The power of her words is still relevant today:

"The child, a free human being, must teach us and teach society order, calm, discipline, and harmony. When we help him, love blossoms, too—the love of which we have great need to bring men together and create a happy life. The aim of education is not to teach facts; education has remained at an absurdly inferior level by comparison with the progress man has made in other fields. I believe that it will seem inconceivable in the near future that education was so narrowly circumscribed that it made the solution of social problems impossible ... The simple truth, as our experience has amply demonstrated, is that the laws the child is forced to obey are arbitrary and that he must no longer be subject to them, so that the laws of life may guide his development. Programs can be changed; the laws of life are immutable, if we base education on the laws of life, we will create genuine levels of education rather than mere curricula" (Montessori, 1949, p. 126).

Word of Dr. Montessori's messages of hope and peace, coupled with her educational pedagogy, reached the ends of the Earth. Soon, her name and ideas were being discussed amongst educators, theorists, and parents throughout the world, marking the beginning of the Montessori Movement. Dr. Montessori laid the groundwork for the inclusion of peace studies in the education of children. Today, more than one hundred years later, research continues to support the need for peace education, both within the Montessori community and the general fields of education and child development (Harris, 2001; Johnson D., Johnson R., 2005; Miller, 2005; Reardon, 1998).

Maria Montessori's voice, message, and writings have been promoting peace education for more than one hundred years. Her belief was that by working with children on conflict resolution, self-control, global awareness, and the fundamental needs of man, the spiritual side of children would be further nurtured and developed. This spiritual development and awareness would ultimately lead to the creation of a new order of peaceful citizens. Montessori's vision is being realized each day through the work of fellow Montessori advocates, nongovernmental organizations (e. g., United Nations, Children's Defense Fund), and educators alike.

There are numerous contexts for providing rich lessons supporting the roots of peace education within the classroom. Although the practices mentioned hereafter have significant positive attributes, their strength can be realized more fully if utilized together. Considering the inclusion of conflict resolution, self esteem building, and cooperative learning, while implementing the goals set forth by the United Nations Manifesto 2000, provides students varied opportunities to experience and practice peace education.

## THE UNITED NATIONS MANIFESTO 2000

The United Nations is one organization promoting peace throughout the world. In fact, Montessori students from around the United States and Canada make annual visits to the UN to inspire global citizenship (American Montessori Society, 2007). The United Nations General Assembly has proclaimed the years 2000–2010 as the Decade for a Culture of Peace and Nonviolence for the Children of the World."As defined by the United Nations, the Culture of Peace is a set of values, attitudes, modes of behavior and ways of life that reject violence and prevent conflicts by tackling their root causes to solve problems through dialogue and negotiation among individuals, groups and nations" (UN Resolutions A/RES/52/13 : *Culture of Peace* and A/RES/53/243, *Declaration and Programme of Action on a Culture of Peace*). This proclamation is summarized in the Manifesto 2000, where people around the world have been invited and encouraged to sign it and take the pledge. More than 75 million signatures have been affixed to the end of this manifesto, each pledging to:

- Respect the life and dignity of each human being without discrimination or prejudice;
- Practice active nonviolence, rejecting violence in all its forms: physical, sexual, psychological, economical, and social, in particular toward the most deprived and vulnerable, like children and adolescents;
- Share time and material resources in a spirit of generosity to put an end to exclusion, injustice, and political and economic oppression;
- Defend freedom of expression and cultural diversity, giving preference always to dialogue and listening without engaging in fanaticism, defamation and the rejection of others;
- Promote consumer behavior that is responsible and development practices that respect all forms of life and preserve the balance of nature on the planet; and
- Contribute to the development of the community, with the full participation of women and respect for democratic principles, in order to create together new forms of solidarity (UNESCO, 2007).

- The goals of this global manifesto can begin to be implemented within the classrooms and schools around the world. The UNESCO Web site provides ample support for teachers by offering lessons and ideas to bring this information to the world's children in a developmentally appropriate way. Additionally, teachers have other ways of promoting the messages put forth through the manifesto. Incorporating global awareness and cultural studies into the regular curriculum, addressing environmental concerns through science, and discussing the universal, fundamental needs of man all assist in supporting the work of the United Nations.

The relationship between Montessori and the work of the UN began at the earliest stages."Montessori was socially active in the forums for world peace. Her *Education and Peace* became the basis of a social movement for peace. An early supporter of the League of Nations and its successor the United Nations, Montessori participated in the foundational meeting of UNESCO, which was tasked with creating the International Institute of Education to promote peace through education" (Barres, 2004, p. 41; Cunningham, 2008, p. 251).

Montessori classrooms around the world continue to support the work of the United Nations by participating in the Montessori Model United Nations."The Montessori Model United Nations Program (MMUN) follows the work of Dr. Montessori to engage students in building peace in the prepared environment of the United Nations, the global forum for peace ... Through the MMUN, the students develop a global political consciousness and take social action by collaborating with Montessori students ... Their energy, commitment, and intelligence—when focused on real work toward a common goal—can help transform the world into one with more peace and justice: a true revolution" (Cunningham, 2008, p. 252).

In addition to supporting the messages of the UN, lessons supporting other aspects of peace education should be considered as well. Meanwhile, setting the tone for these lessons requires some planning and focus. Children must realize that they, too, are important and unique, and that there is a place for them within their communities. Children may begin to see their value through self-esteem building, the class may come together with the strength of a community through the use of cooperative learning activities, and the children within the group may be able to respectfully communicate through the incorporation of a conflict resolution program. These skills and programs are listed as follows:

## Self-Esteem Building

"Educators, parents, business and government leaders agree that we need to develop individuals with healthy or high self-esteem characterized by tolerance and respect for others, individuals who accept responsibility for their actions, have integrity, take pride in their accomplishments, who are self-motivated, willing to take risks, capable of handling criticism, loving and lovable, seek the challenges and stimulation of worthwhile and demanding goals, and take command and control of their lives" (Reasoner, 2008, p. 1). Conversely, children with low self-esteem can exhibit signs of depression and aggression (Waliski, Carlson, 2008, p. 4). The task can seem daunting, and challenging, at first glance. How can educators address all of these concerns and ensure that children are developing a healthy self-esteem?

Teachers may find themselves using these tools from time to time to address specific problems that arise in the classroom, e. g., the exclusion of a particular student, the formation of cliques, hurtful language, etc. Despite these positive intentions, "evidence supports the fact that most schools are not conducive to self-esteem since the level of self-esteem declines for most students the longer they are in school" (Reasoner, 2008). Montessori classrooms have taken an alternate approach.

Montessori environments are designed to eliminate competition. Children are entitled and encouraged to work at their own pace, without the pressure of competing with or comparing themselves to others. Montessori classrooms take a cooperative approach by utilizing multiage classrooms. In multiage classrooms, older children will routinely assist younger children as needed. This form of peer mentoring fosters relationships with others and self-confidence. Teachers must help their children to feel affirmed and valued by the adults in their lives."A child with healthy self-esteem feels loved and capable. Her good feelings about herself will shine through in everything she does. She is likely to take on new responsibilities and try to learn new skills" (University of New Hampshire, 2002, p. 1). Children in Montessori environments increase their classroom responsibilities as they find their sense of place within the classroom community.

As children begin to learn about other world cultures, it is the job of the teacher to help them to understand that their way of thinking, or even a country's way of thinking, is not the only way. There are children's books available to assist in illustrating the lives and sometimes struggles faced by the children of the world. By creating a classroom climate of peace and acceptance, over time, one may find that there is no longer a place for intolerance within that said classroom (Miller, 2005, p. 15).

Montessori teachers may find themselves using some of the books, games, and activities available. However, self-esteem building is more than a unit of study, more than a weekly discussion, and more than a story at circle time. Self-esteem building is visible and practiced on a daily basis within a Montessori classroom. The constant affirmation that each child is a unique and valued member of the classroom community is promoted in every facet of Montessori education.

## COOPERATIVE LEARNING

Cooperative classrooms promote the belief that we are stronger together than alone and that great things can happen when we work toward the common good. Through cooperative learning practices, students work together to solve problems and share experiences."At the heart of cooperative learning theory is the assumption that people learn best from direct experience rather than simply being told information" (Walker, 2006, p. 34). Cooperative learning promotes positive interaction between students and has produced affirmative results."Although much of the research on cooperative learning has been done with older students, cooperative learning strategies are effective with younger children in preschool centers and primary classrooms ... cooperative learning promotes student motivation, encourages group processes, fosters social and academic interaction among students, and rewards successful group participation" (Lyman & Foyle, 1988, p. 1).

Cooperative learning approaches are inclusive of students of all ethnicities, classes, genders, and socioeconomic statuses. The approach stems from three core principals as noted by Jeff Sapp (2006):

- Simultaneous interaction: The more students talk with each other, the more they'll be engaged and the better they'll learn.
- Positive interdependence: The success of every team member is not possible without the success and contribution of each team member.
- Individual accountability: By taking responsibility for a specific portion of the project—and being graded for that—each student becomes individually accountable.
- Montessori included cooperative learning in the design of her classrooms, long before the term was popularized in the 1980s and 1990s by work like Johnson and Johnson's *Cooperation in the Competition: Theory and Research* (1989). Montessori called for multiage classrooms without competition. Children work independently, yet offer assistance and instruction as needed to their counterparts. Older children serve as role models and mentors for younger children in their daily activities and relationships.

Cooperative classroom communities do not occur spontaneously."It stands to reason that a teacher must be committed to the concept of a learning community in order to build one; s/he must also be a caring person and have respect for children and hold certain beliefs about children and how they learn" (Bartel, 2005, p. 151). The teacher builds a classroom community based on trust and respect without the presence of authoritarian practices."Support for this kind of curriculum is found in the standards of the National Council for Social Studies (NCSS) (http:www. socialstudies. org) whose guiding principles for young children include fostering a learning community, developing a democratic classroom, and respecting diversity of thought and culture" (Bartel, 205, p. 152).

Those who have worked extensively in cooperative learning suggest that "cooperative learning should be used when we want students to learn more, like school better, like each other better, like themselves better, and learn more effective social skills" (Johnson, Johnson, Holubec, 1990,

p. 16). Cooperative learning is daily practice in Montessori environments worldwide. Part of learning effective social skills is learning how to solve conflict with grace and courtesy. This, too, is modeled by the teachers, and students, in Montessori classrooms.

## CONFLICT RESOLUTION

Teaching skills for nonviolent conflict resolution need to be modeled and practiced, instilling within children the ability and confidence to use them in their everyday lives. The "I Care Rules" from *Peacemaking Skills for Little Kids* was written by Fran Schmidt and Alice Friedman in the 1980s. Their work has been used by teachers in classrooms around the world to introduce children to the language of peacemaking used in resolving conflict. The authors affirmed that by teaching children active listening skills, children better understand themselves and their environment and come together in creating a sense of community. The "I Care Rules" include: we listen to each other; hands are for helping, not hurting; and we use I-care language. The I-care language may be found on posters within classrooms or above peace tables set aside for the sole purpose of conflict resolution and discussion (Wheeler & Stomfay-Stitz, 2006).

"Although conflict resolution programs are finding acceptance in grade schools, most programs in early care and education have not yet integrated peace-building strategies into their preschool setting" (Vestal, 2004, p. 131). Researchers Myrna Shure and George Spivack concluded that teaching problem-solving skills, or conflict resolution, to young children is a more effective way of guiding children's behavior."Studying children ages 4–12, we learned that regardless of IQ, good problem solvers were less physically and verbally aggressive, were better able to wait and cope with frustration, and were less socially withdrawn. They were also better at standing up for their rights, expressing their feelings, and were more aware of, and genuinely concerned for, peers in distress. These children were more sought out by peers for play or work" (Shure, 2006, p. 10).

Children may seek out a playmate or workmate who has exhibited self-control and the ability to resolve conflict peacefully. Conflicts do arise in early childhood classrooms, and these conflicts, no matter how big or small, can resonate with young children. If a child fears being yelled at, harassed by, or physically threatened by another child due to a conflict, more often than not, they will choose another playmate." Children's success or failure in being accepted by peers is determined in part by their skill in social problem solving" (Waliski & Carlson, 2008). It is safe to assume that a child who lacks these conflict resolution skills could suffer from poor self-esteem as a result of being left out of activities with classmates.

The social development of children is well researched. Three major approaches for building peaceable classrooms include: the development of a child's positive self-esteem, opportunities for cooperative learning, and student and/or peer centered conflict resolution. Montessori classrooms incorporate these approaches on a daily basis.

# Current Research Supporting the Application of Peace Education

In addition to the approaches previously mentioned, there are two themes that are particularly useful in providing a context for educators to develop a peace education curriculum and practice. Multiple Intelligence Theory and Social and Emotional Intelligence are finding their way into educational discussions as well as within the business world (Goleman, 1995, p. xii). The research conducted supports the premise of peace education as well as its preceding applications.

## HOWARD GARDNER: THEORY OF MULTIPLE INTELLIGENCES

Howard Gardner is one of the leading experts in the theory of Multiple Intelligences. MI theory supports the notion of eight intelligences: Linguistic, Logical-mathematical, Musical, Bodily-kinesthetic, Spatial, Interpersonal, Intrapersonal, and Naturalist, with the possibility of a ninth intelligence: Existential (Gardner, 2006). Gardner's theory suggests that every individual possesses each of the intelligences; however, no two individuals will share the same makeup. Although genetics can be shared, life experiences play a role in shaping intelligences, making it impossible to duplicate completely. Exhibiting strength in one of the intelligences does not necessarily suggest that a person has extraordinary intelligence or excels in only one area. For example, a person with a strong linguistic intelligence may spend the day doing crossword puzzles quietly or playing Scrabble with others. A person with a strong mathematical intelligence may spend time calculating the probability of winning the lottery or the slot machines in Las Vegas. Each person will ultimately decide how he or she will use this intelligence and for what purpose, whether it be for the betterment of society or for mere amusement.

Present-day educators may struggle with effectively reaching students whose strengths lie in some of these intelligences and not others. Our current culture places value on language and math skills, and our public schools are faced with teaching to the strengths of the average student toward prescribed curriculum goals. Teachers may not always have the time, leadership, flexibility, or support to present topics to students in a multitude of ways. If they do so, however, Gardner shares that the likelihood of each student in the room grasping the concept at hand increases:

"My research has suggested that any rich, nourishing topic—any concept worth teaching— can be approached in at least seven different ways that, roughly speaking, map onto the multiple intelligences. We might think of the topic as a room with at least seven doorways into it. Students vary as to which entry point is most appropriate for them and which routes are most comfortable to follow once they have gained initial access to the room. Awareness of these entry points can help teachers introduce new materials in ways that can be easily grasped by a range of students, and as students explore other entry points, they can develop multiple perspectives, which are the best antidote to stereotypical thinking" (Gardner, 2006, p. 139).

In an effort to make peace education accessible to a variety of different learning styles, themes of peace education should be made available through a diverse array of materials and lessons. Peace is a concept that can be difficult to describe to young children, especially without a concrete representation. Varied presentations enable the child to visualize peace in numerous contexts. Teaching any subject from one perspective or in the same way time and time again may not reach every child in the room. By incorporating peace education with the Theory of Multiple Intelligences in mind, the likelihood of reaching additional children increases.

"Here is where the idea of multiple intelligences can be of genuine benefit to educators oriented toward the goal of disciplinary understanding. Mastery of a concept or theory requires repeated exposure to that material: one almost never achieves instant understanding. But it is a mistake to present the same content in the same way. Understanding is far more likely to be achieved if the student encounters the material in a variety of guises and contexts. And the best way to bring this about is to draw on all of the intelligences that are relevant to that topic in as many legitimate ways as possible" (Gardner, 2006, p. 60).

A listing of the intelligences and some suggestions for their curricular application as it pertains to peace education is as follows:

- **Linguistic intelligence** involves sensitivity to spoken and written language, the ability to learn languages, and the capacity to use language to accomplish certain goals. Introducing the word *peace* in multiple languages, writing peaceful prose, and reading peace-themed stories are all ways to appeal to the student exhibiting linguistic intelligence.

- **Logical-mathematical intelligence** consists of the capacity to analyze problems logically, carry out mathematical operations, and investigate issues scientifically. The labyrinth math game or using peace symbols as manipulatives are both ways to include peace education in a mathematics area.

- **Musical intelligence** involves skill in the performance, composition, and appreciation of musical patterns. It encompasses the capacity to recognize and compose musical pitches, tones, and rhythms. Providing a CD player with headphones for children to listen to peaceful compositions or nature sounds or the introduction of a basket of instruments to explore appeals to the musical intelligence.

- **Bodily-kinesthetic intelligence** entails the potential of using one's whole body or parts of the body to solve problems. It is the ability to use mental abilities to coordinate bodily movements. Yoga, tai chi, and creative movement can be used to combine peace education with bodily-kinesthetic intelligence.

- **Spatial intelligence** involves the potential to recognize and use the patterns of wide space and more confined areas. Using a Zen garden, whether outside or on a scaled-down version on a tray, is a way to involve spatial intelligence with peace education. Using a finger labyrinth or a full-scale walking labyrinth to walk outside are two additional ways to appeal to this intelligence.

- **Interpersonal intelligence** is concerned with the capacity to understand the intentions, motivations, and desires of other people. It allows people to work effectively with others. Using the peace rose or the peace table to assist in conflict resolution and instilling a culture of grace and courtesy in the classroom honors interpersonal intelligence.

- **Intrapersonal intelligence** entails the capacity to understand oneself and to appreciate one's feelings, fears, and motivations. Yoga, deep breathing, and meditation are various ways to include intrapersonal intelligence in peace education.

- **Naturalist intelligence** is the ability to distinguish and classify objects within the environment. Opportunities to pursue botany, zoology, geology, etc. within the classroom, as well as studies outdoors in nature, would appeal to the naturalist (Gardner, 2007).

Although their research was separated by decades, Maria Montessori and Howard Gardner shared some of their conclusions pertaining to human development. Both came to their theories and conclusions based on the observations and experiences gained through working with children. Gardner and Montessori shared the position that each individual was unique, and strengths and differences were noticeable from the earliest years of life. Montessori writes "little children soon reveal profound individual differences which call for different kinds of help from the teacher" (Montessori, 1964, p. 231). Gardner reasons that "taking human differences seriously lies at the heart of Multiple Intelligence Theory" (Gardner, 1997, 1999; Vardin, 2003, p. 41).

Montessori and Gardner both acknowledged the role environment played in the development of human capabilities."Montessori strongly believed that the child's mind absorbs the environment, leaving lasting impressions on it, forming it, and providing nourishment for it. She warned that the quality of the environment can greatly enhance a child's life or seriously diminish it … Gardner believes that the 'smarter' the environment and the more powerful the interventions and resources, the more competent individuals will become and the less important will be their particular genetic inheritance" (Vardin, 2003, p. 41).

Montessori classrooms, by design, are able to provide learning opportunities related to each of the intelligences. The well-rounded Montessori curriculum includes daily exposure to math, language, music, the arts, nature, and movement, working independently as well as with others. Many, if not most, of Montessori early childhood classrooms serving children ages three to six will have two or three teachers in the classroom each day. These teachers, by the very definition of MI Theory, will exhibit different learning styles and strengths. Children see firsthand that each individual is unique by his or her intelligences and strengths.

## SOCIAL-EMOTIONAL LEARNING THEORY

A second theory useful for providing a framework for peace education is social-emotional learning. It is inevitable that there will come a day when children will turn into the adults of society, filling the roles currently held by adults. It is the role of the educational system to prepare children for this impending responsibility and transfer of the reins. There is debate as to how best to prepare children for this. Some may suggest placing a larger emphasis on math or language instruction as evidenced by the No Child Left Behind Act of 2001. Others may believe that honing problem-solving skills is in order. And still others may feel that the safest bet in preparing children for the future is by educating them about the dangers of drugs and violence. Julia Barrier-Ferreira questions, "What good is it if our students are academically successful, yet lack what is necessary to cope with the more difficult life issues they will face and the interpersonal skills needed to coexist in the global economy for which they are ultimately being prepared?" (2008, p. 139) Although there is much disagreement about the single most important aspect of education, parents, educators, business leaders, and those who shape social policy share the same set of concerns."Schools must become better at guiding children toward becoming literate, responsible, nonviolent, drug-free and caring adults" (Elias, 2004, p. 7).

Social-emotional skills are the skills required to deal effectively with peers and caregivers, as well as the skills necessary to be able to regulate and control emotions. These skills are purposefully taught in schools, with a heightened sense of the importance of modeling responsible reactions to conflict and peers. Some schools have dedicated class time and refer to these skills as a study in self science."The topic, by its very nature, demands that teachers and students focus on the emotional fabric of a child's life—a focus that is determinedly ignored in almost every other classroom in America. The strategy here includes using the tensions and traumas of children's lives as the topic of the day" (Goleman, 1995, p. 261). Self science classes are being taught from first grade through high school in an effort to help young people deal effectively with conflict resolution and the recognition and understanding of underlying emotions."The self science class is a pioneer in the movement that is spreading to schools throughout the country. The names for it range from 'social development' to 'life skills' to 'personal intelligences,' the last referring to the influential model of multiple intelligences put forth by Howard Gardner of the Harvard School of Education" (Goleman, 1993).

Research suggests that when these skills are introduced in classrooms, academic learning improves as well. When academia meets social-emotional learning, students are more likely to retain knowledge and apply it within their lives."They also incorporate into their education a sense of responsibility, caring, and concern for the well-being of others, as well as themselves. Learning thus can be said to touch both the 'head' and the 'heart' and the result is classrooms that are better run and students who are more inspired" (Elias, 2004, p. 3).

Studies in social competence of young children also show its importance in preparing children for attending school."For example, socially competent kindergarteners are more successful than their less competent counterparts in developing positive attitudes about and adjusting to school, and they get better grades and achieve more" (Denham, Blair, DeMulder, Levitas, Sawyer, Auerbach-Major, and Queenan, 2003, p. 239). Confident children, without fear of working with others and with the ability to problem solve, have one less social-emotional barrier to be consumed by."For example, when children enter school with friends, are well liked, are able to make and sustain new friendships, and are able to initiate positive relationships with their teachers, they also feel more positive about school, participate in school more, and achieve more than children who are not described this way" (Denham, et al, 2003, p. 239).

Social-emotional learning is the link that can bridge together academic knowledge with the essential skills needed for success in school and with family, work, and the overall community at large. In a *New York Times* interview with Daniel Goleman, Karen Stone McCown, developer of the self science curriculum at the Nueva School, says, "Learning doesn't take place in isolation from kids' feelings. Being emotionally literate is as important for learning as instruction in math and reading" (McCown, Goleman, 1993).

The International Academy of Education (IAE) is a nonprofit association promoting scientific, educational research, its publication and implementation."The Academy is dedicated to strengthening the contributions of research, solving critical educational problems around the world, and providing better communication among policy-makers, researchers, and practitioners" (Elias, 2004, p. 2). Concerned by the need for the inclusion of social-emotional skills required for enhanced classroom success, the IAE asked the International Bureau of Education to include this research in a series of educational publications to be disseminated.

The International Bureau of Education has developed ten points to consider in regards to social-emotional learning:

1. Learning requires caring.

- Children need to feel cared about and welcomed. The classroom must feel more like a community where each person has value.

2. Teach everyday life-skills.

- Skills that promote self-knowledge, responsible decision making, care for others, and knowing how to resolve conflicts must be taught every day.

3. Link social-emotional instruction to other school services.

- Guidance and counseling services as well as health classes should also incorporate social-emotional learning into their offerings.

4. Use goal-setting to focus instruction.

- Provide children with tools to manage negative emotions and calm themselves down when angry or frustrated. Work together with children to develop goals regarding a particular area or overall classroom contributions.

5. Use varied instructional procedures.

- Use varied approaches to introduce a topic or concept. Refer to Howard Gardner's Theory of Multiple Intelligences for further information.

6. Promote community service to build empathy.

- Provide service opportunities so children can feel they are contributing members of their classroom and their community.

7. Involve parents.

- Involving parents helps to send strong coordinated messages to children. Provide opportunities for parent education, discussion, and exchanges.

8. Build social-emotional skills gradually and systematically.

- Social-emotional learning is not a separate subject area, but instead needs to be incorporated into all aspects of education. This is quite an undertaking, and one which needs to start small before becoming a regular part of school routines.

9. Prepare and support staff well.

- Provide ongoing training, support, and opportunities for professional development for teachers and staff.

10. Evaluate what you do.

- Implement a record-keeping system to evaluate when social-emotional activities take place and their successes or areas that need further refinement. Ask teachers and parents how they will recognize when students' academic and social-emotional skills are improving.

Our children are the greatest asset of society. They will have the daunting task of leading our civilization into the future. Their education is a great responsibility. Within each child lies a great potential, a potential which deserves to be developed. Combining academic and social-emotional learning is a promising way to accomplish the goal of developing the potential within each child.

"In so doing, educators are also preparing students for the tests of life, for the responsibilities of citizenship, and for adopting a lifestyle that is literate, responsible, nonviolent, drug-free, and caring. This is not an easy task. It will require patience as new skills are learned, but not too much patience, as our students are depending on the adults around them to prepare them for their future lives. It is a great responsibility, and it deserves great effort" (Elias, 2004, p. 26).

A clear example of the way social-emotional learning manifests itself within the Montessori classroom can be seen in a video prepared by the American Montessori Society's Peace Committee entitled *Educating for Peace: The Essence of Montessori* (2007). The viewer is taken on a journey through the progression of the Montessori experience, following children from ages twenty months to eighteen years. The video combines clips from the classrooms as well as interviews with teachers and students. The video offers a strong assertion that Montessori classrooms do take the subject of peace education to heart, including self-esteem building, conflict resolution, cooperative learning, and social-emotional learning in their daily practice. The viewer can't help but wonder what might happen if all educational settings were designed to incorporate this into their curriculum but can plainly see that it is, indeed, the essence of Montessori.

# The Montessori Method

It is important to address the prepared Montessori classroom and the lessons and material found therein."There are six basic components to the Montessori classroom environment. They deal with the concepts of freedom, structure and order, reality and nature, beauty and atmosphere, the Montessori materials, and the development of community life" (Polk-Lillard, 1972, p. 51). Within this environment, one will find a number of purposefully arranged child-sized shelves. These shelves will contain the materials originally designed by Montessori, in addition to supplemental materials made or purchased by the trained teacher.

Maria Montessori's educational method, developed more than a century ago, has proved to be timeless in that it continues to address and consider the same concerns modern-day educators ponder in regards to the character development of children. Gardner's MI theory can be recognized in Montessori's lessons (Vardin, 2003, p. 40). Social-emotional learning and its hidden value was also considered by Montessori."Children who are treated with respect and who are encouraged to try new skills learn more readily to do things for themselves. Montessori taught that a child who feels respected and competent will develop a far greater level of emotional well-being than a child who is simply loved and doted upon" (Seldin, 2007, p. 18). These materials will support one of the following areas of the Montessori classroom:

## Everyday Living

The everyday living (a. k. a. practical life) area is often the child's first glimpse of the Montessori classroom. It is designed to be appealing and irresistible to a child. The colors, the textures, the small child-sized tools and materials all beckon for a child to touch and experiment with. It is within this area that the child will be able to work on and master many of the fundamental skills necessary to progress with more advanced Montessori materials.

The four direct aims of the everyday living materials are concentration, coordination, independence, and order. The materials used in this area assist the child in developing these skills in addition to his fine and gross motor control. A strong everyday living area will prove to be an essential element to the overall success of the child's experience within the classroom. This area is attractive to children because they are carrying out familiar tasks that they often see adults doing, like dusting, sweeping, or pouring. The ability to do things independently is a huge motivator for young children, giving them the intrinsic motivation needed to cultivate a genuine love of learning.

There are five main components to the everyday living curriculum: Body Management, Grace and Courtesy, Primary Movements of the Hand, Care of the Person, and Care of the Environment. Each of these areas works within two levels of development. In the first stage, the child exhibits a strong, intrinsic desire to "do it myself." The child works on mastering these skills in an effort to be less dependent of the adults in his world. In the second stage, the child is becoming an active participant in the classroom community, working cooperatively with others, and providing assistance to those who need it (Covington-Packard, 1972, p. 50).

In the Body Management area, children will learn various lessons to help them to move around the classroom with success. They will be shown how to carry a rug to a workspace, unroll it, roll it back up, and return it to its place. They will learn how to carry other objects in the environment as well, from trays to pencils, buckets, and chairs. Other movements necessary are walking on a line, putting on and taking off an apron, and opening and closing a door. These tasks are things we, as adults, often take for granted. However, by breaking these movements down and slowly showing the child how to manage them, we are preparing the child to be able to exist independently within the environment.

With lessons in Grace and Courtesy, the opportunity exists to model for the children how to appropriately respond to social situations by exhibiting grace and courtesy. These lessons are often overlooked in our fast-paced society but are imperative in creating a peaceful learning environment. These lessons in Grace and Courtesy are modeled on a daily basis by the teacher and are often role played for further illustration. These lessons include:

- Speaking with a low voice
- Observing a lesson
- Observing another child at work
- Inviting someone
- Declining an invitation
- Greeting another person
- Saying good-bye
- Excusing oneself
- Waiting to interrupt someone at work
- Asking permission
- Serving food

- Waiting for help from another person
- Offering help to someone
- Introducing someone
- Answering the phone

The Primary Movements of the Hand area is for fine motor control and strengthening the child's hand muscles and grip for writing, in addition to promoting independence, concentration, coordination, and order. Here, the child will be enticed by various activities in scooping, squeezing, twisting, grasping and controlling, rolling and folding, pounding and stringing. The materials are sequenced from large to small, hand to tool, dry to wet, simple to difficult, from left to right across the shelf. Each activity builds on the one preceding it, allowing the child to grow and challenge himself in these areas on his way to mastery. Some of these activities may include:

- Two-hand bead scooping
- Bead scooping/transferring
- Whole-hand sponge squeezing
- Whole-hand basting
- Stirring
- Twisting nuts and bolts
- Pouring pom-poms
- Pouring water with a funnel
- Folding an apron
- Rolling washcloths
- Pounding clay
- Pounding nails
- Stringing napkin rings
- Stringing beads

The Care of the Person sequence fosters a true sense of independence. Here, children will learn self-care lessons allowing them to dress and undress themselves, organize their belongings in an appropriate manner, and tend to personal hygiene. Up until this point, these tasks have typically been the responsibility of the parent or caregiver. In allowing the child the freedom to "do it myself," we provide opportunities for children to practice the very tasks required to do so. In addition to the teacher modeling these lessons, the child has the opportunity to practice independently through the following sequence:

- Dressing frames
    - o Velcro
    - o Button
    - o Snap

- o Zipper
- o Hook and eye
- o Buckle
- o Lacing
- o Bow tying
- Putting on a hat
- Putting on rain boots
- Putting on mittens
- Turing sleeves right side out
- Putting on a jacket
- Hand washing

The Care of the Environment sequence allows the child to help care for the environment of which he or she is a part. Children will learn to clean up spills small and large, dry and wet. They will also learn how to tend to the plants and animals found within their community. These keepers of the environment begin to take pride in and responsibility for the overall care of their classroom, grounds, and planet. Some of the lessons used to practice and hone these skills are:

- Cleaning a large dry spill
- Cleaning a fine dry spill
- Cleaning a wet spill
- Table washing
- Floor sweeping
- Window washing
- Mirror polishing
- Plant watering
- Planting seeds
- Feeding a pet
- Changing an animal cage

The everyday living curriculum provides a framework and a starting-off point for the rest of the curriculum areas. It is here a child will learn the very skills necessary to take any material off of the shelf, organize it, concentrate on the process, manipulate the components, and work with it independently before returning it in the appropriate manner. It is within everyday living that children will learn how to respond to and work with children and adults respectfully and gracefully. Here, children are encouraged to take part in their own self care and the care of the environment around them. The lessons and materials offered here provide children with countless opportunities to develop independence through practical living skills. Additionally, the lessons in grace and courtesy support social-emotional learning and the continued practice of peace education.

## *Sensorial*

Maria Montessori felt that the sensorial area of the classroom was of great importance to the development of the child. It is the area in the classroom designed to assist the child in developing and refining his or her senses. She believed that children are in a formative period between the ages of three and six. Teachers can "assist the development of the senses during this period by graduating and adapting the stimuli to which the child is exposed just as we should assist him in learning how to speak before his speech is completely developed" (Montessori, 1967, p. 143). Sensorial training is one of the basic building blocks of Montessori education. This area provides children with tangible, concrete materials to explore each of the five senses.

"As we know, the period of life extending between the years of three and six is marked by rapid physical growth and the development of the psychic faculties. During these years, a child develops his senses, and his attention is therefore directed toward his environment. He is attracted more by stimuli that will develop his senses rationally and thus lay the foundation for his mental power" (Montessori, 1967, p. 144).

The hands-on work offered in the sensorial area allows for the intellectual development of the child. These materials are intended to be manipulated by children in their efforts to make sense of them. The refinement of their senses assists children in their understanding of the world around them. The direct aims of the sensorial  materials are for the child to observe, compare, contrast, discriminate, reason, decide, make judgments, solve problems, create order, and appreciate the world.

There are five broad categories in the sensorial area. They are: visual, covering size, color, and form; muscular tactile, covering surfaces, textures, temperature, pressure, and stereognostics, which requires visualization through feeling; auditory, covering hearing, distinguishing sounds, and musical tones; olfactory, the sense of smell; and gustatory, the sense of taste. The materials created for these sensorial categories are intended to help children create order, develop senses through simple to complex and concrete to abstract exploration, create deeper understanding by isolating a single quantity, and to broaden perception of the world.

Sensorial materials relate to a child's sensitive period for order. Through using the sensorial materials, a child will learn how to match, sort, and grade, aiding the establishment of order in the child's thought process. The use of sensorial materials "focuses the child's mind on a particular attribute and by an active manipulation leads to a comparison of these objects along the line of that particular attribute. In this way—by working with the different sensorial materials—the child is led to study such qualities as length, breadth, height, color, texture, weight, size, and so forth; and also such geometric forms as squares, triangles, circles, trapeziums, and many others" (Standing, 1957, p. 161).

"The two fundamental concepts to be learned from this kind of apparatus are how to make careful distinctions between similar and different things, and how to grade a set of similar things that differ in a regular and measurable way from most to least. Montessori designed materials for each of the senses in isolation of the others. This makes it possible for a child to experience that he takes in special kinds of information with each of his senses with certain combinations of senses. He can learn basic problem solving and observational strategies, by which materials can be matched or graded, using any of the senses" (Covington-Packard, 1972, p. 35).

Sensorial materials are sequenced on the shelf beginning with the simplest material and moving on to the more complex. This allows the child to build on what he or she has already learned. The sequencing should be as follows: simple to complex, concrete to abstract, left to right, top to bottom, and they should be sequenced by the particular sense that is involved. This area should be set up in close proximity to the mathematics area, as many of the sensorial materials are preparing children for math functions. Children will work with similarities and differences in sensorial, which will then become equalities and inequalities in math.

Most of the sensorial materials are intended to be presented as individual lessons. These lessons should almost always be given first in silence. The teacher may move on and include language at a later date and may present a three-period lesson. In the three-period lesson, the teacher will first tell the child the name of the object. In the second period, the teacher will ask the child to point to the object after the teacher has called out the name. In the third period, the teacher will point to an object and ask the child to recall the name.

The role of the teacher is simply to present the materials to the children so that they may use the materials in an appropriate manner. In addition to ensuring the beauty and completeness of the material, the teacher must also be willing to step back and allow the child to work, explore, and discover without interruption. Materials contain a built-in control of error, allowing the child an opportunity for self-correction.

"As usual, the teacher, by doing the exercises herself, first shows the child how the pieces of each set should be arranged, but it will often happen that the child learns, not directly from her, but by watching his companions. She will, however, always continue to watch the children, never losing sight of their efforts, and any correction of her will be directed more toward preventing rough or disorderly use of the material than toward any error which the child may make in placing the rods in their order of gradation. The reason is that mistakes which the child makes, by placing, for example, a small cube beneath one that is larger, are caused by his own lack of education, and it is the repetition of the exercise which, by refining his powers of observation, will lead him sooner or later to correct himself" (Montessori, 1965, p. 75).

Variations and extensions of the work can be presented when the child has mastered the initial presentation and is ready to move on with the material. A variation allows the child to use the same material in a different manner, while an extension allows the introduction of an additional material to be used as well. Some common variations include: using the materials in a different arrangement; the involvement of other children; or using two or more close-by locations, setting up the material in one location, fetching specific pieces, and transferring them to the second location. Some common extensions include the three period-lesson, using a blindfold, a combination of two different materials, creating a written record, or recognizing the same quality in the environment. By offering the child multiple sensorial experiences and finding comfort in stillness and silence, peace education permeates the sensorial area.

## Math

The mathematical mind has the ability to focus on exactitude and order. Maria Montessori noticed that through the mathematical progress made throughout history, humans needed to qualify, quantify, and classify their experiences. The same might be said for the child's progression through mathematics.

Math skills can be developed with ease by children if presented well and offered the right opportunity. Montessori viewed math as the language for understanding and expressing measurable relationships in our experiences. As early human beings had become proactive, they also became more exact, but the origin for math was always concrete. This process for children is exactly the same. One must start with a concrete experience and move toward the abstract: hand to head. Math can be difficult when we don't give children the opportunity to concretely explore concepts or ideas.

The first instrument to learn how to move and identify our place in space is through the use of the body. Observe young children and see how often they ask us questions pertaining to math, e. g., how much or how many? The sensitive period for math typically occurs between the ages of four and five. Four-year-olds love to count, explore, and question. Math is appealing to the four-year-old because it is constant, it is a comfort, and it is rooted in the concrete. Five-year-olds move toward rational thought and are beginning to want to know what it looks like. They know what a quantity feels like and how we can record it by using numbers (by using pencil and paper).

How does a Montessori classroom prepare a child for math? The well-organized Montessori classroom exhibits a sense of order and predictability. Every material and object has its respective place in the environment and is sequenced from the most basic and concrete presentation to the most complex and abstract. In math, each number has its place, and they, too, are sequenced from the most basic number—one—to numbers with infinite place value. Math is an orderly science, and the Montessori environment speaks to this by way of its design and consistent daily routine. Montessori believed that there was a strong connection between the hand and the mind. In math, children must manipulate materials to gain a clear understanding of how quantities grow or lessen. The Montessori classroom provides ample opportunity and materials for manipulation and exploration. Each area of the Montessori classroom lends itself to the development of the mathematical mind:

- Everyday Living: The activities practiced in the everyday living and sensorial areas set the groundwork for the development of the mathematical mind. Children must have strategies for work, work neatly and precisely, with order and sequence, and learn how to attend to details, all of which is gathered in everyday living. These activities prepare the child for the exactness and logical order for math."A second principle of the Montessori mathematical materials and their presentation is that the child learns, not by looking at or listening to someone else, but by arranging materials in a way that reveals their function and essential ideas" (Covington-Packard, 1972, p. 89).

- Sensorial: "And if we look now at the sensorial apparatus which is able to evoke such deep concentration (remarkable in very young children between the ages of three and four), there is no doubt that this apparatus may be regarded not only as a help to exploring the environment, but also to the development of the mathematical mind" (Montessori, 1967, p. 186). In the Sensorial area, children are working with an experience of 10s. The Sensorial materials isolate one concept at a time, allowing the child to order the experiences. These materials provide a material for abstraction for the concept you want them to acquire. They offer an orderly expression for the concept you want them to learn. The Sensorial area provides a wonderful impression of sets. Geometric solids and the cabinet allows for the exploration of geometry. Cubes relate to work done in geometry and algebra.

- "In an environment prepared according to Montessori's insights, the child's mind has been awakened to mathematical ideas through sensorial experiences. A child has been exposed to experiences that involve precise distinctions of distance, dimension, weight, sequence, plane and solid form, quantity, gradation, identity, difference, sets, units of measurement, ratio, inverse and direct proportion, numerical, algebraic and geometrical progression, congruence, equivalence and similarity. The ideas are not presented theoretically; a child has simply done things with objects that define such ideas. Montessori's sensorial apparatus is an indirect preparation for mathematics for the very young child. The materials designed to develop mathematical concepts also translates abstract concepts into things or actions" (Covington-Packard, 1972, p. 87).

- Language: Language is the script we use. To learn language we use a schema—a script that compartmentalizes information. Children learn math through language and through symbol (orally and symbolically). Language assists children in learning math by:

o   Offering a materialized abstraction of a concept by using manipulatives for exploration;

o   Isolating a specific concept or variables by introducing one concept at a time and building from the most simple example to the more complex;

o   Preparing a child for future knowledge by building on what has already been learned; and

o   Giving the child a mathematical alphabet for the language of math by using the names to the numerals, symbols, and operations.

We have patterns we use for presenting these materials:

o   We introduce quantity;

o   We introduce symbol; and

o   We combine quantity and symbol (association).

o   Children can work with mathematical concepts throughout the classroom without consciously realizing it. In everyday living, there may be ten beads to transfer with a spoon, building the child's understanding of base ten. In sensorial, children can match and sort objects that are the same, developing their one-to-one correspondence. In language, fine motor skills are developed to allow children to record results through writing, graphing, and charting. Additionally, the names of the numerals, symbols, and operations are taught via language. All areas of the Montessori classroom conspire to assist the development of the mathematical mind.

The concrete experiences provided in the math area provide children with a strong foundation to build on as they continue to advance mathematically. The confidence gained through internalizing these lessons directly supports positive self-esteem building in young children.

## Language

A young child's mastery of language must be one of the most amazing, yet overlooked feats of early childhood. To think that toddlers can pick up all of the subtleties and nuances of such a complex language at a time when they are commonly thought to be incapable of learning very much is just fascinating. Maria Montessori recognized this in children and gave them much credit for the very complex observations and comparisons they were able to discern. Through these realizations, Maria Montessori created a rich language curriculum, easily interwoven throughout the other curriculum areas within the classroom.

Training the child for language activities begins in the sensorial area. Here, the child is experiencing the differences among things, whether it is through the discrimination of color, height, weight, sound, or texture. Children are beginning to see, hear, feel, taste, and touch the similarities and differences within their environment.

"Several games invented by Maria Montessori help prepare a child's ear for language. The silence games, in which the children are invited to relax and listen with concentration to the sounds of life ordinarily missed, having a calming effect on the communication efforts of the nervous system. The exercises in matching and grading the sound boxes, which contain objects that make a series of loud and soft noises, or matching an grading the set of bells from high to low pitch, clarify the range of different auditory impulses. Games that isolate and identify individual sounds of nature, noises of mechanical objects, tones of music, or syllables or speech help distinguish the variety of meanings in sounds" (Covington-Packard, 1972, p. 66).

Preparation in Sensorial and Mathematics readies children for further exploration in other areas of the curriculum. By working with the Sensorial and Math materials, the child has been able to create order out of disorder and is beginning to make sense of the things and experiences around him. "He finds himself, therefore, facing the world with psychic qualities refined and quickened. His powers of observation and of recognition have greatly increased. Further, mental images which he has succeeded in establishing are not a confused medley; they are all classified—forms are distinct from dimensions, and dimensions are classed according to the qualities which result from the combinations of varying dimensions" (Montessori, 1965, p. 128).

In helping to prepare a child's ear for language, it is important to introduce the child to new vocabulary whenever possible. Throughout the classroom, there are ever-present opportunities for discussion. Names of continents, countries, animals, plants, foods, etc. are frequently introduced through the various thematic units of study. "The special importance of the sense of hearing comes from the fact that it is the sense organ connected with speech. Therefore, to train the child's attention to follow sounds and noises which are produced to the environment, to recognize them and to discriminate between them, is to prepare his attention to follow more accurately the sounds of articulate language" (Montessori, 1965, p. 123). The teacher must carefully pronounce and annunciate each word to demonstrate for children how words sound and how the mouth looks when forming them. Rhymes, songs, and poems are useful for the teacher to demonstrate proper annunciation.

As with math, at some point, the child will decide that hearing the language is not merely enough: now they hunger to know what it looks like (written word) and how to replicate it (handwriting). Within the carefully prepared Montessori environment, countless materials and activities are designed with the specific aim of preparing the child's hand for writing. Each movement of the hand is isolated and strengthened through distinct everyday living activities. Developing strength in the pincer grip and being able to control the fine motor muscles within the hand are challenging for a small child. Materials to aid in this development can be found not only in everyday living, but in geography with the knobbed map pieces, sensorial with the cylinder blocks, and math with the golden beads. All areas of the classroom come together to help prepare the child for writing right from the start.

"The three fingers which handle the instrument: Three-year-old children remove the cylinders from the solid insets by grasping the knob, which is about the same size as a pen or pencil, with their three fingers. The three fingers thus carry out an exercise that coordinates the motor organs needed for writing a countless number of times.

A light hand: We may observe a child of three-and-a-half as he dips the tips of his fingers into tepid water and, with his eyes blindfolded, devotes his energies toward a single effort, that of moving his lightly poised hand so that the fingers barely glide over the surface of a rough or smooth plane. This effort to move the hand lightly is accompanied by a sharpening of the sense of touch in those fingers which must someday write. In this way the most precious instrument of the human will is constantly perfected.

A firm hand: There is something that precedes the hand's ability to draw a figure; it is the capability of moving it for some specific goal, of being able to guide it in a precise fashion. This ability is a generic property of the hand, since it has reference to the ability to coordinate one's movements or not" (Montessori, 1967, p. 206).

A child's sensitive period for reading typically proceeds the sensitive period for writing. Typically, children are able to write prior to being able to read. The explosion into writing is generally an indication that reading is soon to follow. "Experience has taught me to make a clear distinction between reading and writing, and it has shown me that the two acts need not be absolutely contemporaneous. Our experience, however, has been that writing precedes reading, although this is contrary to what is commonly held. I do not call it reading when a child attempts to verify a word he has written, that is, when he retranslates the symbols into sounds since he already knows the word, having repeated it to many times to himself as he was writing. By reading, I mean the interpretation of an idea by means of graphic symbols. A child who has never heard a word spoken but who recognizes it when he sees it put together on a table in moveable letters and knows what it means, that it is the name of a child, a city, an object, and so forth, really reads. The reason for this is that what is read in writing corresponds to what is heard in speech and is a means of understanding other. A child does not read until he receives ideas from the written word" (Montessori, 1967, p. 229).

The language curriculum, and the breadth of materials supporting its aims, truly speaks to the natural development of the child. It can be humorous to see parents remark about their child's uncanny ability to grasp and control a pencil, wondering how and when they developed such a complex skill. It is at that moment, when the teacher shows the parent all of the countless activities their child has labored over for the past days, month, and years, that the parent will understand why the lessons requiring fine motor control were placed before the child so thoughtfully and persistently from the start.

The language area allows the child to develop a real attention to detail. This focus enables the child to better take in the details of their world. There are four other secondary curriculum areas within the Montessori classroom. These areas complement the core areas of everyday living, sensorial, math and language, but help in giving children a detailed sense of the world around them with all of its culture, music, art and inhabitants. In learning about the world around them, children are more apt to find the similarities between the inhabitants of this ever shrinking world. The seeds of peace education are planted time and time again.

## Geography/Cultural Studies

Geography/cultural studies are covered to illustrate to children not only their place in the world but the similarities and differences amongst the earth's people as well. The aims of this area are to extend the child's knowledge of the world beyond the classroom and their town. Some of the topics and lessons covered in geography include:

1. Land/Air/Water: what they look like, where they are found, animals of each element, modes of transportation, etc.

2. Earth: parts and layers of the planet, land and water forms

3. Continents: both on a map and a globe, names and shapes of each, climate and land forms, animals, flags, etc.

4. Land and Water forms: lake, island, bay, isthmus, cape, peninsula, strait, etc.

5. The aim of the cultural studies component is to introduce and illustrate to children how people around the world live. Each of the seven continents is studied in depth. During the study of each continent, the following may be introduced:

   o Language

   o Music and dance

   o Food

   o Currency

   o Customs, traditions, and holidays

   o Dress

   o Transportation

   o Famous figures

This well-rounded study of each continent is a concentrated effort to not only provide the child with as clear a picture as possible of life in that place, but also to provide multiple entry points to entice each child. Children are completely immersed into the culture of each continent before moving on to the next. By incorporating cultural studies on a daily basis, the differences and commonalities shared, and the study of man over history and time, quite naturally show children their place in the timeline of life. In the end, it is the intention of this curriculum that children will have a better sense of the world around them, the similarities and differences we all share, and the rich cultures of our world.

## Science

The aim of the Montessori science curriculum is to foster a sense of responsibility and appreciation for the planet, as well as to develop the skills to think scientifically, and encourage exploration, observation, and problem solving. Children are provided with lessons and opportunities to experience the beauty of the natural world, as well a means to protect and explore it. Montessorians hold the belief that a hands-on approach is the best way to experience science and develop a scientific mind.

The American Montessori Society suggests that children need the following in regards to a science curriculum:

1. Science experiences matched to the students' developmental needs at all program levels;
2. Development of observation skills for the students, related to nature and natural phenomena;
3. Knowledge of current information in physical and life sciences. Experience with an open-ended array of sequentially organized materials in the physical and life sciences, which empowers students to design their own science projects and activities; and
4. Classroom leadership skills to foster a nurturing environment that is physically and psychologically supportive of learning science curriculum (AMS, 2007).

## Music

Music education in the Montessori classroom can be seen in many forms. As a supplemental area, music can be used to compliment a particular area of study. For example, music is relative to cultural studies. When studying a new continent or country, music from that area may be heard throughout the classroom, indigenous instruments may be found on the music shelf, and native or traditional dances may be presented to the children. Children will further refine their sense of hearing by grading bells by pitch or volume.

Additionally, music appreciation and history are covered within the curriculum. Children are exposed to not only a wide variety of world music, but to classical pieces as well. The lives of composers may be introduced with their musical works. A listening station may be found where children have the opportunity to put on headphones and listen to pieces throughout the day. In some classrooms, soft classical music may be heard playing during the work period.

The elements of music are introduced in a structured way:

1. Rhythm: Echoes, clapping, tapping, etc., encourage the child to associate rhythmic figures with bodily movements.

2. Pitch: Daily singing of songs and finger plays assist the child in developing sense of pitch.

3. Timbre: Orchestral instruments and their classification introduce children to the names of instruments and their various tone qualities.

4. Intensity: Children are exposed to a variety of musical pieces with different gradations of volumes, from a strong march to a soft lullaby.

5. Form: Children begin to realize that music, like language, has a form.

6. Culture: By using music in conjunction with cultural studies, children are better able to relate music to history and geography (AMS, 2007).

## Art

Art in the Montessori classroom can be used to reinforce topics or concepts being presented elsewhere in the classroom. For example, when studying a continent, artists from that continent may be featured in the art area. The artists' medium (paint, clay, or pencil) may be offered for the child's use. Nature studies may prompt art activities using solely natural materials. Lessons in size and shape may inspire a geometric art activity, mosaic, or patterning. Children are shown with great care how to use and manipulate various artistic tools and should decide when to use them and for what purpose. The lessons given in other areas of the classroom might inspire a child to respond in artistic creation.

In the art area, children not only are exposed to a wide variety of mediums for their use, but art history and appreciation as well. Children will be exposed to great masterpieces and artists by matching paintings or sorting pictures by artist or style. Artwork is hung throughout the classroom at the child's eye level, and books are made available depicting various works of art. An art shelf may also be found holding small statues, sculptures, reproductions, jewelry, etc. for the child to explore and observe more intently.

"Art is essential in the environment of the child from birth on. It is a way of approaching life, of moving and speaking, of decorating a home and school, of selecting toys and books. It cannot be separated from every other element of life. We cannot 'teach' a child to be an artist, but we can help him develop: An eye that sees, a hand that obeys, a soul that feels" (Olaf, 2007).

# Incorporation of Peace Education in the Montessori Classroom

Our world has come to a point in time where the promise of a peaceful tomorrow is something we can no longer simply hope for, but instead we have to achieve it for the future of the planet. It is an important responsibility for parents, teachers, and children, as we can undoubtedly shape the course of history. Maria Montessori dedicated her life to creating an educational approach that aimed to follow the child's interests, meet children's developmental needs, provide them with the tools to progress independently, and inspire them to be peacemakers. Her work has touched thousands of children over the course of the past hundred years, with Montessori education often times being cited as one of the agents responsible for the development of conscious global citizens. Her work has inspired present-day educators to pick up the torch and carry on in the pursuit of peace.

## SONNIE MCFARLAND

Sonnie McFarland, a Montessori educator, director, author, and speaker, has made the peaceful education of our children her life's work. She has established herself as one of the leading authorities of peace education in the Montessori world and serves on the American Montessori Society Peace Committee. After decades of observations, she identified the need for educators to have a heightened awareness of how to promote and utilize peace education. McFarland developed a "Flower of Peace" model to help to organize and categorize peace studies. The model includes four areas:

1. Self-Awareness: These activities are designed to help children to experience and appreciate their unique abilities and talents.
   o Everyday Living: Children develop the independence and confidence to maintain their environment and approach their peers with grace and courtesy.
   o Character Education: Children learn about morals and values and will learn about men and women from our history to serve as role models.

- o Consciousness of Self: Children are introduced to the relationship between mind, body, emotional, and spirit.
- o Self-Esteem: Recognize children and their work to assist in creating confident children who are both comfortable and happy.
- o Creative Expression: Provide opportunities for children to express themselves through art, movement, music, etc.
- o Silence Game: This game helps children to find silence and concentrate their thoughts.

2. Community Awareness: These activities are designed to generate understanding and connections within the community.
   - o Grace and Courtesy: Lessons should be used to model respect and manners.
   - o Cooperative Learning: Children learn to work with and appreciate peers.
   - o Communication Skills: Children are provided with the tools and language needed for expression.
   - o Problem Solving: Create a separate space for peer problem solving, like a peace table, peace corner, etc.
   - o Acknowledgments: Use concrete symbols to illustrate thoughtful or helpful actions within the classroom.
   - o Conscious Community Building: The environment must be safe and respectful so that a child can feel heard and understood, ultimately developing strong personal identities.
   - o Community Service Learning: Provide opportunities for participation in community service projects.

3. Cultural Awareness: These activities generate cross-cultural appreciation and recognition.
   - o Cosmic Education: Define basic human needs and help children realize how these needs are met (or are not met) throughout the world.
   - o Multicultural Study: Children learn about all aspects of various world cultures through stories, music, artwork, games, food, etc.
   - o Cultural Exchanges: Children enjoy classroom guests, speakers, musicians, etc., or having pen pals from another country.
   - o Celebrations: Host classroom and school-wide international celebrations.
   - o Study of the United Nations: Discuss the work of the UN in spreading peace.
   - o Diversity Training: Model acceptance of persons different than ourselves.

4. Environmental Awareness: These activities highlight the interconnectedness of all living things and the fragility of the planet.
   - o Cosmic Education: Create stewards of the earth.
   - o Scientific Study: Learn about the elements of the earth and the "web of life."

o Study of the United Nations: Discuss the work the UN has done in preservation of the earth's natural resources.

o Ecological Activities: Actively include children in caring for the environment, e. g., gardening, recycling, composting, etc.

o Environmental Celebrations: Classroom and school-wide celebrations and projects centered on Earth Day (McFarland, 1999, p. 31–35).

Children often learn more by what they see than what they hear. It is imperative that teachers and the adults who work with children model peace, grace, and courtesy. It is through observing these behaviors that children are more likely to adopt them as their own. In order for teachers to be able to approach each day with peace and poise, they must continue to work on their own spiritual preparedness. Maria Montessori felt this was equally as important and had the following to say:

"The first essential is that the teacher should go through an inner, spiritual preparation—cultivate certain aptitudes in the moral order. This is the most difficult part of her training, without which all the rest is of no avail … She must study how to purify her heart and render it burning with charity toward the child. She must 'put on humility.' And above all, learn how to serve. She must learn how to appreciate and gather in all those tiny and delicate manifestations of the opening life in the child's soul. Ability to do this can only be attained through a genuine effort toward self-perfection" (Standing, 1957, p. 298).

# Conclusion

At this point in history, educators who espouse Montessori, Gardner, and Goleman's work, among others, are beckoned by a call to peace. It is through their work that hope may exist in creating a new world of peace, justice, and equality. Many steps have been taken, important steps undoubtedly. Until peace education can be found in every school, is placed on political agendas, and becomes a field of scientific inquiry, there remains work still to be done."Preventing conflicts is the work of politics; establishing peace is the work of education. We must convince the world of the need for a universal, collective effort to build the foundation for peace" (Montessori, 1949, p. 27).

This curriculum was prompted by the significant body of work done by Dr. Maria Montessori (1949, 1964, 1965, 1967). Her educational pedagogy and the environmental design of Montessori classrooms served as the foundation for this project. Montessori began telling the world in the 1930s that the education of young children needed to focus on their spiritual development if we were ever to see peace in our world."In order to do this, all nations would have to reach an understanding, to bring about a sort of truce that would permit each of them to devote itself to the cultivation of its own human members in order to find therein the practical solutions to social problems that today seem insuperable. Perhaps the attainment of peace would then be easy and close at hand" (Montessori, 1949, p. 31).

In an international effort to promote peace and nonviolence for the world's children, the United Nations proclaimed the years 2000–2010 as the Decade for a Culture of Peace and Nonviolence for the Children of the World. This measure directly supports the groundwork laid by Maria Montessori and its present-day applications. Montessori schools continue to support this work by taking part in the Montessori Model United Nations each year (Cunningham, 2008).

This curriculum takes into account several peace education programs and approaches used in recent history: self-esteem building (Reasoner, 2008), cooperative learning (Johnson, Johnson, & Holubec, 1990), and conflict resolution (Wheeler & Stomfay-Stitz, 2006). The essence of these programs, while not specifically named, may be found within the Montessori curriculum and philosophy. While there remains value in using these approaches in a supplementary manner (Bartel, 2005; Sapp, 2006; Vestal, 2004; Walsiki & Carlson, 2008), Montessori recognized the impact they might have when used together on a daily basis in a cooperative, supportive, and inclusive classroom environment.

*The Friendly Classroom for a Small Planet* (Prutzman, Stern, Burger, 1988) was a groundbreaking book dealing primarily with conflict resolution and community building with young children. Johnson and Johnson prepared a text to assist teachers in teaching these skills to young children (Johnson and Johnson, 1991). Betty Reardon, director of the Peace Education Program of Teachers College at Columbia University, wrote *Educating for Global Responsibility* (Reardon, 1988); however, only sixteen pages of the book were dedicated to lessons written for the early childhood population.

Realizing that peace education extends beyond the sole skill of conflict resolution, other authors have published books and articles in support of this work. Books like *Sensational Meditation for Children* (Wood, 2006) and *Baby Buddhas* (Desmond, 2004) supported teachers in introducing meditative practices to young children. There has been no shortage of books written about yoga for children (Buckley, 2006; Lark, 2003; Stewart & Philips, 1992), and studios are frequently adding children's classes or parent-child classes to their schedules.

Still, finding one curriculum written for the express purpose of reaching the early childhood population is difficult at best. In researching the significant importance of including social-emotional learning in the classroom, it was self-evident that these lessons and skills needed to be made accessible to all students regardless of learning style, ethnicity, gender, ability, or socioeconomic status. By relying on the thorough research conducted by Howard Gardner and his Theory of Multiple Intelligences (2006), lessons were created aimed to inspire peace in children regardless of where their intelligences or interests may lie. These lessons were written for children served in early childhood settings, which are oftentimes a child's first exposure to school.

The purpose of this work is to provide all teachers, not solely those within Montessori environments, with another set of tools to add to their repertoires. Although this book was written with the Montessori classroom in mind, other settings can incorporate these practices into any program serving an early childhood population. By continuing to present the themes, ideas, and processes conveyed through peace education in new and exciting ways, teachers will be better able to reach the early childhood population. In spreading this message of peace and hope to the young children of our world, teachers provide them with the opportunity and encouragement to go out and become peacemakers capable of achieving unknown possibilities. The fate of humanity is indeed in the hands of our children. It is our job to provide our children with the strength they will need and the tools they are bound to require to sow the seeds of peace for a bountiful future.

# Part Two:
# The Curriculum

# Introduction

Welcome to *Pathways for Peace: Lessons to Inspire Peace in the Early Childhood Classroom.* These lessons have come to fruition through my work as a Montessori teacher and parent. As a parent, one of my main goals is to help guide my children into becoming caring and responsible citizens. I realize the value of a rich academic education, yet I also want to be sure that my children are capable of understanding their emotions and handling them as well, and that they are able to work effectively with others. High marks on tests at school are well and good, but I am equally as proud when I watch my five-year-old daughter assist a young three-year-old with the task of zipping her jacket, or when my six-year-old facilitates conflict resolution between two quarrelling friends. These are the skills I believe will serve them best when out in the world. These are the skills I try to nurture both within my home and within the classroom as well.

The lessons provided herein are aimed to introduce some of the themes and symbols of peace through a variety of ways. I have written these lessons keeping Howard Gardner's Theory of Multiple Intelligences in the back of my mind, as well as the principles and practices of Maria Montessori. By combining these two philosophies, I have been able to create Montessori-style lessons speaking to each of the eight intelligences. It is my sincere hope that by introducing this important information in a variety of ways, more teachers will be able to access it and use it effectively to help children gain important skills and understanding.

Each lesson is structured with ease of presentation in mind. The format mirrors lesson plans typically written by Montessori teachers. As is expected in the Montessori classroom, we begin with a concrete example of a subject before progressing to the more abstract. I encourage you to begin by showing the children concrete examples of the symbols of peace. Provide a peace dove, a labyrinth, or a mandala. Allow these symbols to be integrated throughout your environment. At the same time, use the lessons in grace and courtesy to help promote and model peaceful interactions within your environment. The more children work with symbols of peace and receive peaceful messages, the more likely they are to see these symbols and actions within their world.

A white bird will never be simply a white bird for my daughter again. A sighting of a white bird has now become a sighting of a peace dove, and it brings peace to her each time it appears.

I hope the lessons within this curriculum provide you with a renewed sense of peace and inspire you to help nurture the next great peacemakers of our world. In working with these lessons, remain conscious of how the children react. Are they involved and excited or withdrawn and uninterested? Did you have to modify any part of the lesson? Was there one lesson in particular the children simply loved? I would love to hear from you with any comments, suggestions, or personal stories you might be willing to share. Please look at the end of this work in the Resources section to find a listing of books, CDs, Web sites, and training programs that will assist you and complement this work. Thank you for joining me in this valuable work. In the words of Maria Montessori: "To help children become aware of the love that rests inside each one of them is, I feel, one of the most important aspects of nurturing spirituality and teaching peace" (Wolf, 1996, p. 121).

**Name of Activity:**  Silence Game

**Area:** Sensorial/Auditory

**Materials:** None needed

**Aims:** To observe, compare, contrast, discriminate, reason, decide, solve problems, make judgments, create order and appreciate the world; to appreciate internal and external silence.

**Presentation:**

1.  Ask each child individually if he or she would like to play the silence game.
2.  If yes, invite the child to join group in circle. If no, engage child in alternate activity with teacher away from the group.
3.  Say, "Today we will make silence. Silence is when we keep our bodies still and we don't make any sounds."
4.  Wiggle fingers.
5.  Make fingers still and silent.
6.  Wiggle toes.
7.  Make toes still and silent.
8.  Shake head.
9.  Make head still and silent.
10. After two minutes, call each child softly by name, in a whisper.
11. When child hears his name, he will rise silently and go noiselessly to the teacher.
12. Silence game is only over after each child has been called by the teacher.

**Variations and Extensions:**

1.  Turn off the lights and play lying down.
2.  Set up as an individual work with a sign the child may place in front of them reading, "I am being silent."

**Name of Activity:** The Bell Game

**Area:** Practical Life/Body Management

**Materials:** Small hand bell, 6–8 inches in length

**Aims:** Concentration, self-control, centering

**Presentation:**

1. Gather children together in a circle. Tell them you are all going to play a game together. Tell them that for this game you have to absolutely silent. To be absolutely silent, you must not speak or move around. Even our clothes can make noise! For this game, we are going to try to pass the bell all the way around the circle without ever hearing it ring. If we do hear it ring, the game will be over and we'll have to try again another day. Let's see how far we can make it around the circle today.

2. The teacher begins with the bell placed on the floor directly in front of her. Slowly lift the bell by the handle using a three-finger pincer grip. Gently place the bell on the floor in front of the child to your left (or right, depending on which direction you opt to move. ) The child will then pick the bell up in turn and place it in front of his neighbor, and so an and so forth until you have either made a full rotation or heard the bell.

**Variations and Extensions:**

1. Organize children into a line and have them take turns carrying bell across the room and back.

2. Ask children to sit in a circle with their eyes closed. One child will walk around the outside of the circle with the bell and quietly place it on the floor in front of a friend without being heard. Ask the children to open their eyes. The child who discovers he or she has received the bell will then have a turn to walk around the outside of the circle.

**Name of Activity:**   Brain Dance

**Area:** Practical Life/Body Management

**Materials:** None needed; may elect to use lively instrumental music

**Aims:** To warm up the body, centering activity

**Presentation:**

1. This is a group activity. Ask children to stand up in their spaces. Begin by tapping: tap your heads, faces, ears, chests, backs, arms, stomachs, legs, every part of you body all the way down to your feet. Proceed to squeezing, squeezing every part of your body from head to toe. Conclude with brushing, brushing every part of your body from head to toe. *Note: this should be a fun and lively activity with the teacher being quite animated.

2. Experiment with movements that move from the center out, e. g., hunch down into a little ball, and explode into a giant X shape with arms and legs outstretched.

3. Play with movements that bring the head and tail together, curving forward, backward and side to side.

4. Move only the upper part of your body (waving arms, reaching high, etc. )  then move only the lower half (marching, knee bends, etc. ).

5. Alternate between moving only the left side of the body and the right side.

6. *Spin*! Spin in one direction for fifteen seconds. Rest for fifteen seconds. Spin in the opposite direction for fifteen seconds. Rest and breathe.

**Variations and Extensions:**

1. Use this to begin the day or before you want the children to give you their undivided attention. Also can be used prior to yoga. Experiment with various ways to move the body.

**Name of Activity:** Creating Shapes

**Area:** Practical Life/Body Management

**Materials:** None needed

**Aims:** Concentration, coordination, independence

**Presentation:**

1. 1. This activity should be done in a group. Gather children in a circle, ensuring each child has ample room to stretch out their body without touching their neighbor. (You may place felt circular dots on the floor to outline where the children should sit)

2. Tell the children," Today we will each have a chance to create a new shape using our bodies. Our shapes will not move. They must stay still. After you show us your new shape, we will all try to make our bodies do the same thing."

3. Teacher enters the middle of the group and creates a new shape by holding a pose.

4. Ask children if they would like to try to make that shape.

5. Teacher returns to place in circle.

6. Invite another child to enter the middle of the group to make a new shape.

7. Children continue to use their bodies to create new shapes until everyone has had a turn.

**Variations and Extensions:**

1. Children can create their shapes in a dedicated area of the classroom and a teacher or friend may draw that pose on an index card using stick figures. The child can then name their new shape or pose.

2. You can also create movements in a small enough group.

**Name of Activity:**  Talking With a Low Voice

**Area:** Practical Life/Grace and Courtesy

**Materials:** None needed

**Aims:** To model how to speak quietly to another person

**Presentation:**
1. "Today we are going to have a lesson on how to talk with a low voice."
2. "To talk with a low voice means to speak quietly."
3. "Let's pretend that I am a child and Mary is a child. I am going to talk to her with a low voice."
4. Mary sits down next to me at the table. We speak quietly to each other.
5. Ask the children: "What did I do?  How did I do it?  Why did I do it that way?"
6. Ask if anyone else would like to volunteer to try.
7. Debrief.
8. Repeat steps 6–7 several times.

**Variations and Extensions:** None

**Name of Activity:** Observing a Lesson

**Area:** Practical Life/Grace and Courtesy

**Materials:** None

**Aims:** To model how to observe a lesson

**Presentation:**

1. "Today we are going to have a lesson on how to observe someone's lesson."
2. "To observe a lesson means to watch with your eyes silently."
3. "Let's pretend that I am a child and Mary is a child. Susan is going to give Mary a lesson, and I am going to observe the lesson."
4. Susan presents lesson to Mary while I sit nearby watching silently without touching the work or interrupting the lesson.
5. Ask the children: "What did I do? How did I do it? Why did I do it that way?"
6. Ask if anyone else would like to volunteer to try.
7. Debrief.
8. Repeat steps 6–7 several times

**Variations and Extensions:** None

**Name of Activity:**   Observing Another Child at Work

**Area:** Practical Life/Grace and Courtesy

**Materials:** None needed

**Aims:** To model how to observe another child at work

**Presentation:**

1. "Today we are going to have a lesson on how to observe another child at work."
2. "To observe another child at work means to watch with your eyes silently. "
3. "Let's pretend that I am a child and Mary is a child. Mary is going to do her work and I am going to observe her at work."
4. Mary works with materials at a mat and I sit nearby watching silently without touching the work or interrupting the child.
5. Ask the children: "What did I do?  How did I do it?  Why did I do it that way?"
6. Ask if anyone else would like to volunteer to try.
7. Debrief.
8. Repeat steps 6–7 several times.

**Variations and Extensions:** None

**Name of Activity:** Inviting Someone

**Area:** Practical Life/Grace and Courtesy

**Materials:** None needed

**Aims:** To model how to invite another person

**Presentation:**

1. "Today we are going to have a lesson on how to invite someone."
2. "To invite someone means to ask someone to do something."
3. "Let's pretend that I am a child and Mary is a child. I am going to invite her to have snack with me."
4. I approach Mary and ask, "Mary, would you like to have snack with me?"
5. Ask the children: "What did I do? How did I do it? Why did I do it that way?"
6. Ask if anyone else would like to volunteer to try.
7. Debrief.
8. Repeat steps 6–7 several times.

**Variations and Extensions:** None

**Name of Activity:** Declining an Invitation

**Area:** Practical Life/Grace and Courtesy

**Materials:** None needed

**Aims:** To model how to decline an invitation

**Presentation:**

1. "Today we are going to have a lesson on how to decline an invitation."
2. "To decline an invitation means saying no when someone asks you to do something and you do not want to. Decline an invitation."
3. "Let's pretend that I am a child and Mary is a child. Mary is going to invite me to have snack with her and I am going to say, 'no.' I am going to decline her invitation."
4. Mary approaches me and asks if I would like to have snack with her. I say, "No, thank you."
5. Ask the children: "What did I do? How did I do it? Why did I do it that way?"
6. Ask if anyone else would like to volunteer to try.
7. Debrief.
8. Repeat steps 6–7 several times.

**Variations and Extensions:** None

**Name of Activity:** Greeting Another Person

**Area:** Practical Life/Grace and Courtesy

**Materials:** None needed

**Aims:** To model how to greet someone

**Presentation:**

1. "Today we are going to have a lesson on how to greet another person."
2. "To greet another person means to say hello."
3. "Let's pretend that I am a child and Mary is a child. I am going to greet her."
4. Mary enters the classroom and I say, "Hi, Mary. Good morning!"
5. Ask the children: "What did I do? How did I do it? Why did I do it that way?"
6. Ask if anyone else would like to volunteer to try.
7. Debrief.
8. Repeat steps 6–7 several times.

**Variations and Extensions:** none

**Name of Activity:**   Saying Good-bye

**Area:** Practical Life/Grace and Courtesy

**Materials:** None needed

**Aims:** To model how to say good-bye

**Presentation:**

1.  "Today we are going to have a lesson on how to say good-bye."
2.  "Let's pretend that I am a child and Mary is a child. I am going to say good-bye to her."
3.  Mary and I walk toward the door together and I say, "Good-bye, Mary. See you tomorrow!"
4.  Ask the children: "What did I do?  How did I do it?  Why did I do it that way?"
5.  Ask if anyone else would like to volunteer to try.
6.  Debrief.
7.  Repeat step 5–6 several times

**Variations and Extensions:** None

**Name of Activity:**   Waiting to Interrupt Someone at Work

**Area:** Practical Life/Grace and Courtesy

**Materials:** None needed

**Aims:** To model how to interrupt someone at work

**Presentation:**

1. "Today we are going to have a lesson on how to interrupt someone at work."
2. "Interrupting someone at work means getting their attention when they are busy with their work."
3. "Let's pretend that Mary is a child and I am a child. I am going to interrupt her while she is working."
4. Mary sits down at a mat to work on a material. I approach her from behind and gently place my hand on her shoulder. Mary continues with her work and then acknowledges me and says, "Thanks for waiting for me to finish my work. What did you want to tell me?"
5. Ask the children: "What did I do?  How did I do it?  Why did I do it that way?"
6. Ask if anyone else would like to volunteer to try.
7. Debrief.
8. Repeat steps 6–7 several times.

**Variations and Extensions:** None

**Name of Activity:** Asking Permission

**Area:** Practical Life/Grace and Courtesy

**Materials:** None needed

**Aims:** To model how to ask for permission

**Presentation:**

1. "Today we are gong to have a lesson on how to ask permission."
2. "Asking permission means to ask if you may do something."
3. "Let's pretend that I am a child and Mary is a child. I am going to ask her if I may look at the book she brought to school. I am going to ask permission."
4. I approach Mary and ask, "Mary, may I please look at the book you brought to school today?" Mary replies, "Yes, you may."
5. Ask the children: "What did I do? How did I do it? Why did I do it that way?"
6. Ask if anyone else would like to volunteer to try.
7. Debrief.
8. Repeat steps 6–7 several times.

**Variations and Extensions:** None

**Name of Activity:**   Waiting for Help from Another Person

**Area:** Practical Life/Grace and Courtesy

**Materials:** None needed

**Aims:** To model how to wait for help from another person

**Presentation:**

1. "Today we are going to have a lesson on how to wait for help from another person."
2. "Let's pretend that I am a child and Mary is a teacher. I need Mary's help and I am going to wait for her to help me."
3. Mary is writing something at the counter. I ask her if she could please help me to zip my sweater. Mary says, "Yes, I will help you as soon as I finish writing this." I stand patiently and wait for her to finish her work before she helps me.
4. Ask the children: "What did I do?  How did I do it?  Why did I do it that way?"
5. Ask if anyone else would like to volunteer to try.
6. Debrief.
7. Repeat steps 5–6 several times.

**Variations and Extensions:** None

**Name of Activity:** Offering Help to Someone

**Area:** Practical Life/Grace and Courtesy

**Materials:** None needed

**Aims:** To model how to offer help to someone

**Presentation:**

1. "Today we are going to have a lesson on how to offer help to someone."
2. "Offering help to someone means to ask someone if they would like you to help them to do something."
3. "Let's pretend that Mary is a child and I am a child. Mary just spilled her snack on the floor and I am going to offer to help her clean up."
4. Mary spills her snack on the floor. I ask, "Mary, would you like me to help you to clean up your snack?" Mary says, "Yes, please." We clean up the snack together.
5. Ask the children: "What did I do? How did I do it? Why did I do it that way?"
6. Ask if anyone else would like to volunteer to try.
7. Debrief.
8. Repeat steps 6–7 several times.

**Variations and Extensions:** None

**Name of Activity:** Introducing Someone

**Area:** Practical Life/Grace and Courtesy

**Materials:** None needed

**Aims:** To model how to introduce someone

**Presentation:**

1. "Today we are going to have a lesson on how to introduce someone."
2. "Introducing someone means telling someone who doesn't know a person their name."
3. "Let's pretend that I am a child, Mary is a child, and Susan is my mom. I am going to introduce Mary to my Mom."
4. Susan and I are standing together and Mary approaches us. I say, "Mom, this is my friend Mary. Mary, this is my mom."
5. Ask the children: "What did I do? How did I do it? Why did I do it that way?"
6. Ask if anyone else would like to volunteer to try.
7. Debrief.
8. Repeat steps 6–7 several times.

**Variations and Extensions:** None

**Name of Activity:**   Scooping Doves

**Area:** Practical Life/Primary Movement of the Hand

**Materials:** Two one-inch square crystal salt dishes, one containing ten dove-shaped eyelets, and a 1. 5-inch long crystal salt spoon, positioned on a tray

**Aims:** Concentration, coordination, independence, order. Scooping doves into two small bowls. Recognition of the peace dove.

**Presentation:**
1.  Using pincer grip of dominant hand, grasp scoop.
2.  Raise spoon.
3.  Position spoon above dish of doves.
4.  Rotate wrist counterclockwise 180 degrees so that the spoon is facing the left-hand side of the tray.
5.  Lower spoon to the bottom of the dish of doves.
6.  Slowly slide one dove onto spoon.
7.  Rotate wrist clockwise 180 degrees so that spoon is facing skyward.
8.  Position spoon with dove over second dish.
9.  Rotate wrist counterclockwise 180 degrees, dropping dove into dish.
10. Repeat steps 2–9 until all doves have been transferred into second dish.
11. Admire work.
12. Repeat steps 2–8 until all doves have been returned to original dish.
13. Replace spoon to center of tray with handle facing midline.
14. Place hands in lap.
15. Admire work.

**Variations and Extensions:**
1.  For a beginning activity, use larger materials to include larger doves, etc. for scooping.
2.  Scoop doves out of salt with a slotted spoon.

**Name of Activity:** Planting Peace

**Area:** Practical Life/Grasping and Controlling

**Materials:** Wooden planter-shaped stand with 5-1/8 inch holes bored into top, five wooden wands with circular disks, and 1/8-inch shafts painted blue and bearing peace symbols.

**Aims:** Concentration, coordination, independence, order, recognition of peace symbols

**Presentation:**

1. Using pincer grip of dominant hand, grasp one wand by the shaft, just beneath the circular disk.
2. Raise wand above planter.
3. Position base of shaft vertically above open hole on planter.
4. Slowly slide wand into open hole in planter.
5. Release wand.
6. Repeat steps 1–5 until all wands have been inserted into planter.
7. Using pincer grip of dominant hand, grasp one and remove it from planter.
8. Gently return wand to tray.
9. Release wand.
10. Repeat steps 7–9 until all wands have been returned to tray.
11. Place hands in lap.
12. Admire work.

**Variations and Extensions:**

1. Spell *peace* by painting one letter on each disk.

**Name of Activity:**   Pushpin Labyrinth

**Area:** Language/Preparation of the Hand

**Materials:** Piece of construction paper with labyrinth design drawn or printed; corkboard or mat; pushpin or stylus

**Aims:** To acquire a mastery of the hand through the lightness of touch and by keeping within the limits provided; recognition of the labyrinth

**Presentation:**

1. Give the following instructions: "The push pinning work is for one child and must be used at a table. Please be careful with the pushpin because it is sharp. Push pins may only be used to punch holes in paper."
2. Child places paper on top of rug or mat.
3. Child traces outline of labyrinth using two fingers of dominant hand.
4. Punch out shape by perforating outline with a pin.
5. Child now has a tactile, perforated labyrinth to trace with finger as needed.

**Variations and Extensions:**

1. Outline various other pictures or shapes for child to push pin.

**Name of Activity:**   Common Pin Buttons

**Area:** Practical Life/Primary Movements of the Hand

**Materials:** A small tray containing a 5x5 photo frame with glass removed and three layers of cork glued inside, containing five heart-shaped buttons in a row, with a corresponding set of five smaller identical heart-shaped buttons positioned in a row beneath the first. A small box containing twenty common pins, positioned to the left of the corkboard on the tray.

**Aims:** Concentration, coordination, independence, order

**Presentation:**
1. Using dominant hand, grasp lid of box.
2. Raise dominant hand above tray, removing lid from box.
3. Place lid of box in top left corner of workspace.
4. Using pincer grip of dominant hand, reach into box.
5. Grasp ball of one common pin.
6. Lift dominant hand from box.
7. Position pin above first buttonhole on the top left button of corkboard.
8. Lower common pin into buttonhole.
9. Push common pin into corkboard.
10. Release common pin.
11. Repeat steps 4–10 until all common pins have been inserted into buttonholes, moving from left to right across board.
12. Admire work.
13. Using pincer grip of dominant hand, grasp one common pin, removing it from corkboard.
14. Gently return common pin to box.
15. Release common pin.
16. Repeat steps 13–15 until all common pins have been returned to box.
17. Using dominant hand, grasp lid of box.
18. Replace lid on box.
19. Place hands in lap.
20. Admire work.

**Variations and Extensions:**
1. Use other peace-themed buttons.
2. Arrange buttons in the shape of a peace symbol.

**Name of Activity:**   Peace Tree

**Area:** Everyday Living/Grasping and Controlling

**Materials:** Small, artificial tree with boughs; assorted ornaments with ribbons for hanging

**Aims:** Coordination, concentration, independence, order

**Presentation:**

1.  Remove tree from basket.
2.  Stand tree in center of workspace.
3.  Remove one ornament from basket.
4.  Thoughtfully select a bough to hang the ornament on.
5.  Thread bough through ribbon on ornament, hanging it on tree.
6.  Continue with remaining ornaments until all have been hung on tree.
7.  Admire work.
8.  Remove ornaments one at a time and return them to basket.
9.  Return tree to basket.

**Variations and Extensions:**

1.  Dedicate a tree outside as the peace tree and allow children to decorate.

**Name of Activity:**   Stringing Peace

**Area:** Practical Life/Stringing

**Materials:** Ten ceramic peace-symbol beads and a 12-inch length of leather cord with a wooden bead tied at the end, arranged on a tray

**Aims:** Concentration, coordination, independence, order, stringing, recognition of peace symbol

**Presentation:**

1. Grasp one bead with nondominant hand.
2. Pick up end of cord using pincer grip of dominant hand.
3. Position opening of bead at start of cord.
4. Using dominant hand, slowly thread cord through hole in bead.
5. Grasp end of cord with subdominant hand as it pushes through the bead.
6. Slide bead to the beaded end of cord with dominant hand.
7. Repeat steps 1–6 with remaining beads.
8. Remove beads, one at a time, replacing them in tray.
9. Roll cord up and replace in tray.
10. Admire work.

**Variations and Extensions:**

1. Use other peace-themed beads.
2. Use multiple bead designs to create a pattern.
3. Place pattern cards on the tray for child to replicate with beads.

**Name of Activity:** Peace Crane Matching

**Area:** Sensorial/Visual

**Materials:** One small dish containing ten sets of matching laminated picture cards. The sets are as follows: peace signs, the word *peace*, the peace crane, hand peace sign, olive branch wreath, ancient Asian peace symbol, Chinese character for peace, Japanese character for peace, Hebrew character for peace, and the Islamic character for peace.

**Aims:** To observe, compare, contrast, discriminate, reason, decide, solve problems, make judgments, create order and appreciate the world, perceive identities, recognize international peace symbols.

**Presentation:**
1. Place dish in center of rug.
2. Remove one card from the dish, placing on the rug to the right of the dish.
3. Repeat step 2 until all cards have been placed on the rug in controlled random order.
4. Place dish in the top left corner of the rug.
5. Pick up one card and look at it closely.
6. Place the card below the dish at the top left corner of the rug.
7. Pick up another card from the right-hand side of the rug.
8. Compare the card with the card previously placed beneath the dish. If it doesn't match, shake head no, and place card beneath first. If it does match, shake head yes, and place the card to the right of the match.
9. Repeat steps 7–8 until all remaining cards have been matched.
10. Admire your work.
11. Return dish to the center of the rug.
12. Return cards to the dish, one at a time, from top to bottom, left to right.

**Variations and Extensions:**
1. Use other symbols.
2. Use object instead of cards.
3. Play a distance game by having child set up two rugs at opposite ends of the room. Place card in controlled random order on one rug, and begin matching on the second rug.

**Name of Activity:**   Peace Symbol Sorting

**Area:** Sensorial/Visual

**Materials:** Five each: peace symbols, suns, trees, doves, "love"

**Aims:** To observe, compare, contrast, discriminate, reason, decide, solve problems, make judgments, create order and appreciate the world, perceive identities, recognize peace symbols.

**Presentation:**

1. Place bowl in center of rug.
2. Remove one object from the bowl.
3. Set object down on the rug to the right of the bowl.
4. Repeat steps 2–3 until all objects are set on the rug to the right of the bowl in controlled random order.
5. Move bowl to the top left-hand corner of the rug.
6. Pick up one object and place it to the right of the bowl along the top of the rug.
7. Pick up another object and compare it to the first object placed at the top of the rug. If it does not match, shake head no, and begin a new category by placing it to the right of the object. If it does match, shake head yes, and place object directly beneath the match.
8. Repeat step 7 until all objects have been sorted.
9. Admire your work.
10. Return bowl to the middle of the rug.
11. Return objects to the bowl one at a time, from left to right.

**Variations and Extensions:**

1. Sort objects directly from the bowl.

**Name of Activity:**   Peace Dove Grading

**Area:** Sensorial/Visual

**Materials:** Five peace doves differing in size

**Aims:** To observe, compare, contrast, discriminate, reason, decide, solve problems, make judgments, create order and appreciate the world, perceive identities, contrasts, and sequential quantity.

**Presentation:**
1.  Place basket in center of rug.
2.  Remove doves, one at a time, placing to the right of the basket in controlled random order.
3.  Place basket in top left-hand corner of rug.
4.  Place largest dove beneath the basket at the top left-hand corner of the rug.
5.  Place smallest dove next to the largest dove, isolating the extremes.
6.  Return the smallest dove to controlled random order.
7.  Visually identify the next largest dove and place gently to the right of the largest dove.
8.  Repeat step 7 until all doves have been graded from largest to smallest.
9.  Admire your work.
10. Place basket in center of rug.
11. Return doves to the basket one at a time.

**Variations and Extensions:**
1.  Grade from smallest to largest.
2.  Grade while blindfolded.
3.  Place doves in controlled random order on one rug, and carry doves one at a time to another rug across the room and arrange from largest to smallest.

**Name of Activity:** Labyrinth Math Game

**Area:** Math

**Materials:** One game board depicting a labyrinth with flowers in its path, a dove pawn, dice

**Aims:** Counting, one-to-one correspondence

**Presentation:**

1. This game is for one player, just as walking the labyrinth is something we do alone.
2. Player rolls the dice and counts the dots.
3. Player picks up dove and advances said amount of spaces.
4. Player repeats process, rolling, counting, advancing, until the center of the labyrinth is reached.
5. Player repeats process in reverse, moving from the center of the labyrinth back out from the entrance.

**Variations and Extensions:**

1. Draw a labyrinth with chalk outside and have child move himself around the labyrinth.

**Name of Activity:**   Can You Say Peace?

**Area:** Language/Cultural Studies

**Materials:** *Can You Say Peace?* by Karen Katz, globe, outlined continent map, preprinted list of the word "peace" translated in a variety of languages

**Aims:** Seeing peace globally, hearing new languages

**Presentation:**

1. Read the book *Can You Say Peace?* by Karen Katz to the children in a group setting.
2. Look at either a globe or a map and point out the continents and various countries.
3. Show the children an outlined continent map.
4. Remove the list of peace translations and cut the first one off the top.
5. Read it to the children and the name of the country.
6. Locate the country on the map and glue the label on the map.
7. Continue cutting, locating, and labeling for remaining translations.
8. Have a master copy laminated and available on the tray to serve as a control of error for the child.

**Variations and Extensions:**

1. Have a word of the day in a different language posted in the classroom and refer to it often.

peace

United States

*paz*

Mexico

*mojjsa kamana*

Bolivia

*paix*

France

*goom-jigi*

Ghana

*mir*

Russia

*sohl*

Iran

*shanti*

India

*he ping*

China

*heiwa*

Japan

*kurtuku*

Australia

**Name of Activity:** The Peace Dove

**Area:** Cultural Studies

**Materials:** A palm-sized peace dove (often found in the floral or wedding section of craft stores), placed in a basket or nest

**Aims:** To introduce the child to the international symbol of the peace dove

**Presentation:**

1. Group activity to be done in a circle.

2. In a small basket, place a hand-sized peace dove, covered with a beautiful fabric, so as not to let the children see it. Discreetly peer inside the basket, showing the children joy on your face as you see what is inside. Tell the children that you have brought something very special to share with them today by saying the following.

3. "If you were to travel all around the world, it might be difficult to communicate at times because there are so many different languages spoken. There is a symbol, though, that is known throughout the entire world. You could travel to India, Antarctica, Spain, Japan, or anywhere at all, and no matter where you were, the people around you would know that this symbol represents peace. Does anyone have any ideas about what that might be?"

4. "I brought a symbol of a peace dove today." Slowly and tenderly remove the peace dove from the basket and cup in your hands as if it were extremely fragile. Begin to speak in a whisper. Tell the children that only the gentlest hands may receive the peace dove. After admiring the dove in your hands, slowly and carefully pass the peace dove to the outstretched hands of the child next to you. Allow that child sufficient time to admire the dove prior to passing it on to the next child.

**Variations and Extensions:**

1. The basket may then be placed on the shelf as an activity for the children to focus or concentrate in silence.

**Name of Activity:**   Peace Dove Memory Game

**Area:** Language

**Materials:** Set of twenty laminated photo cards comprised of ten pairs of representations of peace doves.

**Aims:** To see similarities and differences, matching, memory work

**Presentation:**

1.  This is a game for two children.
2.  On a mat between the two children, all of the cards will be turned over and arranged in a square formation.
3.  The first child will choose two cards to turn over, revealing the picture on the opposite side. If the two cards are the same, the child can keep the pair and repeat his turn. If they are not the same, the cards must be turned back over.
4.  Emphasize to the children that it is their job to try to remember what those cards were. The next child will now have a turn to flip two cards over.
5.  The game continues until all of the matching pairs have been found.

**Variations and Extensions:**

1.  You can create this game with virtually any symbols or words.

**Name of Activity:** Three-Part Yoga Cards

**Area:** Language

**Materials:** Three-part yoga cards for the following poses: rock, star, child, downward-facing dog, seated wide angle, boat, snake, tree, mountain, stork, crane

**Aims:** To introduce the child to various yoga postures both visually and by name; to further the child's exposure to the written word and to provide continued reading practice

**Presentation:**

1. Using three-part cards, lay out first set of card with labels attached, reading each one as you place it from left to right across mat.
2. Using photo set of cards, match to each photo in the first set, placing directly below the match.
3. Using label set of cards, read and match to the proper photo, placing directly below match.
4. Prior to putting away, teacher shows child each photo card asking child to imitate the pose and say the name. *Or,* prior to putting away, teacher shows child each label, one at a time and away from the photos, asking child to read each of them.

**Variations and Extensions:**

1. Picture cards can be left in a basket in a corner of the room where children can roll out a mat and practice yoga.
2. Blank paper with a pencil can be placed in a basket where children can either draw, or have a friend draw, a new yoga pose they have discovered, complete with new name.
3. The name of the "Pose of the Day" can be posted in the classroom for children to read and then try the pose.

**Name of Activity:** The Peace Mandala

**Area:** Art/Cultural Studies/Math

**Materials:** Examples of mandalas, mandala coloring books, mandala maker (found in craft or specialty toy stores), stencils for design purposes

**Aims:** To introduce the child to the peace mandala and link it to various aspects of life. To allow the child to work with and create peace mandalas.

**Presentation:**

1.  Group activity to be done in a circle.
2.  "The word *mandala* is Sanskrit for 'whole world' or 'healing circle.' Mandalas are historically used as symbols to help people meditate, and for protection and healing rituals. Mandalas can be simple or complex circular designs which tend to draw the eye inward to the center. Mandalas can be found almost everywhere, in nature, design, science, and art."
3.  Show various examples of mandalas.

**Variations and Extensions:**

1.  Have templates of mandalas available for the child to color.
2.  Either invest in a Mandala Maker or provide stencils and guides for children to experiment with designing their own mandalas.
3.  Helpful resources: *Kids' First Mandalas* by Sterling Publishing Co. ; http://www. papermandalas. com/resources. htm

**Name of Activity:** The Peace Crane

**Area:** Cultural Studies/Art/Yoga

**Materials:** Origami peace crane

**Aims:** To share the story of Sadako and the Thousand Cranes, to introduce the crane as a symbol of peace, to experience the crane yoga posture

**Presentation:**

1. Group activity to be done in a circle.
2. Recite story: "Sadako Sasaki was two when a United States bomber dropped an atomic bomb on Hiroshima. She died ten years later of radiation-induced leukemia. In the hospital, she began folding a thousand paper cranes (the white crane is the sacred bird of Japan, and one hundred origami cranes traditionally mean the granting of a wish). Her friends asked children in Japan and thirteen other countries to make a contribution to a memorial in Hiroshima's Peace Park, which was set up in 1958 with the words 'This is our cry, this is our prayer, to build peace in the world' inscribed on its base. In the 1980s, students of the International School, looking for a way to keep this message of peace alive, set up the 1000 Crane Club; they produced a booklet and asked groups of children worldwide to become members by sending one thousand paper cranes for Sadako's memorial. The first response came from an American school in 1986. Children, almost entirely unaided, had started a movement and established a globally recognized symbol of hope for peace." (www. sadako. org)
3. Show the children a folded peace crane, letting them know that children around the world have folded hundreds and thousands of these cranes to be placed at the Peace Park in Hiroshima. Ask them if they have seen these peace cranes anywhere else.
4. It is a bit difficult to fold these cranes; there is another way we can make a peace crane. We can make peace cranes through yoga. There is a yoga posture called the peace crane. Demonstrate.

**Variations and Extensions:** Note: The instructions are included if you have children who would like to attempt to fold a peace crane, most likely with assistance.

**Name of Activity:** The Labyrinth

**Area:** Sensorial/Math

**Materials:** A finger labyrinth, a maze

**Aims:** To introduce the labyrinth as a peaceful practice; to see different kinds of labyrinths: finger labyrinth, walking labyrinth, labyrinth in art, etc.

**Presentation:**

1. This is a group activity to be done in a circle. Explain to the students:
2. "A labyrinth looks like a maze, but is not. A maze is like a puzzle to be solved. It has twists and turns and dead ends. You have to think and think and be alert for any clues you may find. A maze can be frustrating, frightening, or challenging. You can get lost in a maze."
3. "A labyrinth, unlike a maze, has no dead ends. There is only one path, and while it does have twists and turns, you can't get lost. The same path takes you into the labyrinth and out again. With a labyrinth, you don't have to think, or analyze, or solve a problem. With a labyrinth, you just trust that the path will lead you to where you need to be."
4. Provide children with a simple maze to trace. Notice how many children experience getting lost by making a wrong turn. Next, offer them a three-circuit labyrinth and have them trace it. Notice that no one gets lost. Ask about the difference between a maze and a labyrinth. Point out that you can't get lost in a labyrinth. There are no wrong turns.
5. Provide finger labyrinth on the shelf for children to work with.

**Variations and Extensions:**

1. Take children to an outdoor labyrinth, or construct one.
2. Using a large piece of canvas, paint a labyrinth for the children to walk inside.

**Name of Activity:** Peace Notes

**Area:** Language/Art

**Materials:** Various card-making materials, envelopes, stamps, ink pads, pencils, ribbon, glue, various embellishments

**Aims:** To give children the opportunity to send their peaceful messages out into their world

**Presentation:**

1. Ask children if they have received a card from a friend or from someone in their family before. Was it for a holiday or a special occasion? How did it make them feel when they received it? Were they surprised?

2. Ask children if they have ever sent or given a card to a friend or family member before. Did they buy it at the store, or did they make it themselves? How did it feel to choose it or make it? What kind of message did it contain?

3. Tell children that today we will have an opportunity to make a card for someone we know. But, it's not a holiday. Peace is something we can celebrate each and every day, without having a special holiday. Peace is a message we can share with our friends and family every single day.

4. What kind of messages might we add to our peace cards? What kind of pictures or symbols might we use? What kinds of things remind us of peace? (Answers may vary. )

5. Set up a card-making center at a small private table, with various card-making materials, envelopes, stamps, ink pads, pencils, ribbon, glue, embellishments, and examples of some peaceful words: peace, love, hope, friend, hello, etc.

**Variations and Extensions:**

1. Contact another Montessori school, either locally or internationally, and set up a peace-card exchange, showing that peaceful messages can be received and given around the world.

**Name of Activity:** The Helping Book

**Area:** Language

**Materials:** Blank, unlined journal in a basket with some colored pencils

**Aims:** To have a year long classroom project, to have a visual representation of the help we have offered and received

**Presentation:**

1. Place a blank journal in a basket with some colored pencils.
2. As a class, discuss the ways children have been helped throughout the day or the week.
3. Encourage them to illustrate people helping them in the pages of the journal. Those who are writing can also write about it.
4. Keep the journal on the shelf for the year, encouraging the children to add to it when they wish in an effort to create a class "Helping Book."

**Variations and Extensions:**

1. Create a "Book of Solutions." When conflict arises between two children, they may come to the teacher with the Book of Solutions. In this journal, the teacher can help the children to record the problem. Both parties may then offer solutions to be recorded as well. At the end, the solution they have compromised upon and chosen should also be recorded. At the end of the year, the book can serve as a reminder of the peaceful solutions and conflict resolution process we used.

**Yoga and Creative Movement: Class Outline**

**Warm Up/Brain Dance**

1. Tap body from head to toes.

2. Squeeze body from head to toes.

3. Brush body from head to toes.

4. Hello in there (bend at the waist with legs spaced wide apart, waving between legs to those behind you) / Hello out there (stand up tall and wave high in the sky)

5. Big *X* (standing up, create an *X* with your body, stretching your arms high and wide, with a wide stance) / Little *O* (crouch down toward the ground, making your body into a small ball)

6. Spread peanut butter on one foot, jelly on the other. Slap them together and bend down to eat!

7. Lizard crawling up wall: quickly and in slow motion. (Imagine a wall in front of you. Place your hands against it. Slowly pretend to crawl up that wall with your hands and your knees, begin to move more quickly, and end in slow motion. )

8. Swing arms in different directions: high/low, left/right, front/back

9. March in place/simple knee bends

**Yoga Postures**

1. Introduce three new yoga poses using the three-period lesson by using poses found in yoga books, a yoga deck, or from your own experience.

**Movement**

1. Introduce three new movements with music: skipping, running, walking, hopping, flying, swimming, crawling, slithering, sliding, etc. ; be creative!

**Peace Education**

1. Read a book or introduce a concept or symbol.

**Relaxation**

1. Inhale and raise hands above head; exhale and lower hands.

2. Say with children, "May we have peace in our bodies, peace in our minds, and peace on our hearts."

3. Say with children, "*Shanti, shanti, shanti*. Peace, peace, peace."

4. Explain meaning of the word *namaste*. Have children bow to each other and say *namaste*.

**Ideas for Group Activities:**

- When calling children to group or circle, silently crouch down in the rock pose or child's pose. It will only take moments before most if not all of the children see what you are doing and imitate you. This has proven to be a silent and stress-free transition to group time.

- Start your day or group time with some of the Brain Dance exercises to help children to release some energy and regain focus.

- Make up your own yoga poses!

- Link poses and movement to curriculum. For example:

- When studying weather, how can our movements be like a lightning bolt? How can we be like soft rain?

- When studying a continent or country, move to its music.

  - When learning about trees, talk about what it would feel like to be a strong redwood. What about a young sapling? What would it look like in the fall when the leaves float to the ground?

  - Move like the animals you study.

  - Pose like the statues you see in art.

# Conclusions

This curriculum provides a wide scope of activities pertaining to and supporting each of the distinct learning styles discussed in Gardner's MI theory. While many of the curricula currently made available to teachers provide well-thought and meaningful lessons, they often cover one aspect of peace education, or present it in a singular manner. There are books upon books about conflict resolution, children's yoga, or self-esteem. Unlike these books, the aim of this curriculum is to be inclusive of a wide variety of theories and disciplines with materials intended for group discussion as well as independent work cycles.

The strength of this curriculum lies in the fact that it encompasses lessons designed for each of the multiple intelligences. The lessons were expressly written for the developmental level of children between the ages of three and six. Since this was written solely for the early childhood setting, these lessons do not have to be tailored or pared down for their application. However, these lessons can be enhanced to serve elementary students as well.

The weakness of this curriculum is that it requires the teacher to create many materials to effectively present the lessons. This may not only be time-consuming, but costly if working within a strict budget. There are not directions provided for the development of these materials, and they may not be self-evident to those unaccustomed to materials development. This curriculum caters to the Montessori educator and may prove to be arduous to others.

Although this particular curriculum was originally written for use within the Montessori community, it certainly should be considered for other venues as well. Religious education programs may find that the peaceful messages found therein complement some of their teachings. Traditional school programs may be able to use the lessons under their character education programs. The yoga and movement sections could be included in physical education classes.

One teacher I spoke to uses meditation in her classroom under the title of "concentration skills." Labyrinths are being used to help pediatric cancer patients at the Texas Children's Hospital.

This curriculum was written for all children and has the potential for being implemented in schools, religious education programs, after-school programs, summer camps, and more. The possibilities have no bounds. These lessons are created simply so that they may be useful in many different settings.

While there are many different types of educational training programs, seminars, and workshops available, none of them is a prerequisite for using these lessons. If there is a desire to take these lessons even further, to another, deeper level, then some additional training may be found valuable, insightful, and hopefully inspiring. After watching my children fall in love with yoga, I soon realized they were looking for more than I was able to provide. After taking an introductory teacher's training program, I was better equipped to design fun, thoughtful lesson plans that really encouraged and spoke to my class. It has been my experience that each workshop I have attended that related to children, spirituality, or peace education has resulted in the formation of at least ten new ideas to be used within the classroom. I find that by maintaining my professional development, I am able to recharge my batteries and give new life to old lessons, or create new lessons from the information and inspiration I have received. Resources for various training programs and professional development opportunities may be found in the resources section of this work.

This curriculum is a starting point for the introduction of peace studies in the early childhood program or home. The more comfortable the teacher is with the material, the more effective the presentation will be. Observe children. See what they respond to and find ways to add to it. If, after presenting several lessons in yoga, children are clamoring for more, consider weekly or monthly yoga classes either at a studio or held within schools. There is a vast array of literature, programs, and articles that support what teachers do and enhance curriculums. As professionals, we can work together with our colleagues to generate ideas and share resources in the spirit of spreading and promoting peace.

Parents and educators may note that this work has affected children at various times and situations. I like to say, "We will see it when it counts." My own children have been raised hearing about peace every day. There are times when they even tire of hearing me talk about it. But their art contains pictures of children holding balloons with peace symbols on them, skies full of peace doves, and clean fields and meadows full of flowers. My daughter will reach for a finger labyrinth and trace it repeatedly in her room when she feels the need to calm herself down. I have watched my daughter champion the rights of a younger classmate, coming to her defense when the youngster was too overcome with emotion to speak. I hear my children question certain positions held by political candidates, wondering if these politicians really will protect their vision of a peaceful world. I find my children interested in the lives of peacemakers in our history and watch them simply beam with pride when they, too, are referred to as peacemakers. For these reasons, and countless others I have witnessed through my own children and those I serve, I know that peace education works. I see how peace can manifest itself within the hearts of children. And I believe that this work—the work of harboring peace within our children—is the most meaningful, and ultimately, powerful work I will ever know.

# Resources

**Parent/Teacher Education:**

Bartlett, J. *Parenting with Spirit: 30 Ways to Nurture Your Child's Spirit and Enrich Your Family's Life.* New York: Marlowe and Company, 2004.

Carlsson-Paige, N. *Taking Back Childhood: Helping Your Kids Thrive in a Fast-paced, Media-saturated, Violence-filled World.* New York: Hudson Street Press, 2008.

Carlsson-Pagie, N. *Before Push Comes to Shove: Building Conflict Resolution Skills with Children.* St. Paul, MN: Redleaf Press, 1998.

Daleo, M. *Curriculum of Love: Cultivating the Spiritual Nature of Children.* Charlottesville, VA: Grace Publishing & Communications, 1996.

Dermond, S. *Calm and Compassionate Children: A Handbook.* Berkeley, CA: Celestial Arts, 2007.

Hart, T. *The Secret Spiritual World of Children.* Novato, CA: New World Library, 2003.

Lancer, B. *Parenting with Love … Without Anger or Stress.* Atlanta, GA: GDG Publishing, 2007.

Levin, D. *Teaching Young Children in Violent Times: Building a Peaceable Classroom.* Cambridge, MA: Educators for Social Responsibility, 2003.

McConnell, C. (ed. ) *Making Peace: Healing a Violent World.* Bainbridge Island, WA: Positive Futures Network, 2003.

McFarland, S. *Shining Through: A Teacher's Handbook on Transformation.* Buena Vista, CO: Shining Mountains Press, 1993.

Reardon, B. (ed. ) *Educating for Global Responsibility: Teacher Designed Curricula for Peace Education, K–12.* New York: Teachers College, Columbia University, 1988.

Wolf, A. *Nurturing the Spirit in Non-sectarian Classrooms.* Holidaysburg, PA: Parent Child Press, 1996.

http://exchanges. state. gov/Forum/Journal/peace. htm

www. tolerance. org

http://wilderdom. com/games/PeaceEducationExperientialActivities. html

**Stories for Children:**

Baskwill, J. *If Peace is …* New York: MONDO Publishing, 2003.

Bass, J. *Peace, Love and Vegetables (Herb the Vegetarian Dragon).* Barefoot Books: Cambridge, MA, 2005.

Berkeley, L. *The Seeds of Peace.* Cambridge, MA: Barefoot Books, 1999.

Bloom, B. *Crackers.* New York: Orchard, 2000.

Boritzer, E. *What is Peace?* Los Angeles, CA: Veronica Lane Books, 2006.

Carlson, N. L. *How to Lose All Your Friends.* New York: Puffin, 1997.

DeRolf, S. *The Crayon Box that Talked.* New York: Random House, 2000.

Garrison, J. *A Million Visions of Peace: Wisdom from the Friends of Old Turtle.* New York: Scholastic Press, 2001.

Gilley, J. *Peace One Day.* New York: Putnam Juvenile, 2005.

Katz, K. *Can You Say Peace?* New York: Henry Holt and Company, 2006.

Kerley, B. *A Little Peace.* New York: National Geographic Children's Books, 2007.

Lalli, J. *Make Someone Smile.* Minneapolis, MN: Free Spirit Publishing, 1996.

Leaf, M. *The Story of Ferdinand.* New York: Scholastic, 1984.

Lionni, L. *Swimmy.* New York: Knopf, 1963.

Meek, A. & Massini, S. *I'm Special, I'm me!* New York: Scholastic Books, 2005.

Munson, D. *Enemy Pie.* San Francisco: Chronicle, 2000.

Nickle, J. *The Ant Bully.* New York: Scholastic, 1999.

O,Neill, A *The Recess Queen.* New York: Scholastic, 2002.

Radunsky, V. *What Does Peace Feel Like?* New York: Atheneum Books, 2003.

Scholes, K. *Peace Begins with You.* San Francisco, CA: Sierra Club Books, 1989.

Tafuri, N. *Will You be My Friend?* New York: Scholastic, 2000.

Williams, S. *Talk Peace.* New York: Holiday House, 2005.

Wolf, A. *Our Peaceful Classroom.* Holidaysburg, PA: Parent Child Press, 1991.

**Yoga and Movement:**

Baptiste, B. *My Daddy is a Pretzel.* Cambridge, MA: Barefoot Books, 2004.

Buckley, A. *The Kids' Yoga Deck.* San Francisco, CA: Chronicle Books, 2006.

Lark, L. *Yoga for Young People.* New York: Sterling Publishing, 2003.

Pla, A "El lado mas bestia de la vida." On *Cover the World: World Music Versions of Classic Pop Hits* [CD]. New York: Putumayo World Music, 2003.

Norian, T. "Heart Space." On *Deep peace* [CD]. Pittsfield, MA: Mike McAvoy, 1996.

Stewart, M. & Phillips, K *Yoga for Children.* New York: Fireside Books, 1992.

Wiseman, W. & Dajani, S "Good good good." On *Bodywise* [CD]. Canada: Kidzup Productions, 1996.

**Mandalas:**

Verlang, A. *Kid's Mandalas.* New York: Sterling Publishing, 2004.

Verlang, A. *Kid's First Mandalas.* New York: Sterling Publishing, 2005.

http://www. chinaberry. com/prod. cfm/pgc/11800/sbc/11802/inv/5486/tid/805121206

**Labyrinths:**

Bartnett, B. *Peace Labyrinth: Sacred Geometry.* Ruidoso, MN: Lifestyle Institute, 1995.

McCarthy, M. *Kids on the Path: A Manual for Bridging the Labyrinth Experience to School Children.* Santa Fe Schools, 2007. Retrieved March 13, 2007 from www. labyrinthresourcegroup. org.

http://ispiritual. com

www. labyrinthonline. com

**Meditation**:

Desmond, L. *Baby Buddhas: A Guide for Teaching Meditation to Children.* Kansas City: Andrews McMeel Publishing, 2004.

Viegas, M. *Relax Kids: Aladdin's Magic Carpet and Other Fairytale Meditations for Children.* United Kingdom: O Books, 2004.

Wood, S. *Sensational Meditation for Children.* Asheville, NC: Satya Method Resource Center, 2006.

www. mindworksforchildren. com

**Workshops, Conferences, and Training:**

American Montessori Society: www. amshq. org

Association Montessori International: www. montessori-ami. org/

Child Spirit Institute: www. childspirit. org

Kripalu: Center for Yoga and Health: www. kripalu. org

Moving Spirit: Center for Yoga Dance and Wellness: www. movingspirityogadance. com

North American Montessori Teachers' Association: www. montessori-namta. org/NAMTA/ index. html

Peace Games: www. peacegames. org

Sensational Meditation for Children: www. sarahwood. com

The Montessori Foundation: www. montessori. org

The Alternative Education Resource Organization: www. educationrevolution. org

Vermont Peace Academy: www. vermontpeaceacademy. org

# References

Ajmera, M., Verala, A., Global Fund for Children. *Children from Asia to Zimbabwe: A Photographic Journey Around the World.* Watertown, MA: Charlesbridge Publishing, 2001.

American Montessori Society. *Educating for Peace: The Essence of Montessori.* [DVD]. Yellow Springs, OH: Educational Video Publishing, 2007.

American Montessori Society. *Position Paper on Science Education.* 2007. Retrieved October 31, 2007 from http://www. amshq. org.

American Montessori Society. (2007). *Position Paper on Music Education.* 2007. Retrieved October 31, 2007 from http://www. amshq. org.

Barres, V. Maria Montessori and UNESCO. *AMI Communications.* 2004: #2–3, 41–44.

Barrier-Ferreira, J. "Producing Commodities or Educating Children? Nurturing the Personal Growth of Students in the Face of Standardized Testing." *The Clearing House.* (2008): 81–83, 138–140.

Bartel, V. "Learning Communities: Beliefs Embedded in Content-based Rituals." *Early Childhood Education Journal.* 33:3. (2005): 151–154.

Berne, P., Savary, L. *Building Self-esteem in Children.* New York: Crossroad Classic Publishing, 1999.

Blood, M. *I CAN DO IT! Positive Self-esteem Songs for Kidz.* [CD]. CA: Musivation, 2004.

Buckley, A. *The Kids' Yoga Deck.* San Francisco, CA: Chronicle Books, 2006.

Copsey, S., Kindersley, B. *Children Just Like Me.* New York: DK Publishing, 1995.

Covington-Packard, R. *The Hidden Hinge.* Notre Dame, IN: Fides Publishers, Inc., 1972.

Cunningham, J. (2008)."The Montessori Model United Nations." *NAMTA Journal 33* (2008): 249–257.

Daleo, R. *From a Grain of Sand: Happiness.* [CD]. Cambridge, MA: Mindworks for Children, 2001.

Denham, S. A., Blair, K., DeMulder, E., Levitas, J., Sawyer, K., Auerbach-Major, S., & Queenan, P. "Preschool Emotional Competence: Pathway to Social Competence?" *Child Development 74* (2003): 238–256.

Desmond, L. *Baby Buddhas: A Guide to Teaching Meditation to Children.* Kansas City, MO: Andrews McMeel Publishing, 2004.

Elias, M. *Academic and Social-emotional Learning.* 2004. Retrieved December 13, 2007 from http://www. casel. org.

Gardner, H. *Extraordinary Minds.* New York: Basic Books, 1997.

Gardner, H. *Intelligence Reframed: Multiple Intelligences for the 21st Century.* New York: Basic Books, 1999.

Gardner, H. *Multiple Intelligences.* New York: Basic Books, 2006.

Goleman, D. *Emotional Intelligence.* New York: Bantam Books, 1995.

Goleman, D. "Managing Your Feeling 101." *The New York Times.* 1993. Retrieved March 1, 2008 from http://query. nytimes. com/gst/fullpage. html?res=9F0CEFD9153CF934A35752 C1A965958260

Harris, I. *Challenges for Peace Educators at the Beginning of the Twenty-First Century.* Milwaukee, WI: Department of Educational Policy and Community Studies, 2001.

Hollyer, B. *Wake Up World! A Day in the Life of Children Around the World.* New York: Henry Holt & Co., 1999.

Johnson, D., & Johnson, R. (2005)."Essential Components of Peace Education." *Theory into Practice*, 44(4):280. Available from: ERIC, Ipswich, MA. Accessed on August 25, 2007.

Johnson, D., Johnson R., & Holubec, E. *Cooperation in the Classroom*. Edina, MN: Interaction Book Co., 1990.

Johnson, D. W., & Johnson, R. *Cooperation and Competition: Theory and Research*. Edina, MN: Interaction Book Company, 1989.

Johnson, D., & Johnson, R. *Teaching Students to be Peacemakers*. Edina, MN: Interaction Book Company, 1991.

Lark, L. *Yoga for Young People*. New York: Sterling Publishing, 2003.

Levin, D., & Carlsson-Paige, N."Sowing the Seeds of Nonviolence." *Education Week* (1998): 31.

Lyman, L., & Foyle, H. "Cooperative Learning Strategies and Children." *ERIC Digest*. Urbana, IL: ERIC Clearinghouse on elementary and early childhood education, 1988.

McFarland, S. "Nurturing the Peace Flower: A Model for the Science of Peace." *Montessori Life 11* (1999): 31–35.

Miller, S."Building a Peaceful and Just World—Beginning with the Children." *Childhood Education 82* (2005): 14–18.

Montessori, M. *Education and Peace*. Chicago, IL: Henry Regnery Co., 1949.

Montessori, M. *The Montessori Method*. New York: Shocken Books, 1964.

Montessori, M. *Dr. Montessori's Own Handbook*. New York: Shocken Books, 1965.

Montessori, M. *The Absorbent Mind*. New York: Holt, Rinehart, Winston, 1967.

Montessori, M. *The Discovery of the Child*. New York: Ballantine Books, 1967.

Mosley, J., & Sonnet, H. *101 Games for Self-esteem*. Wisbech: LDA, 2002.

Olaf, M. *Child of the World*. 2007. Retrieved October 31, 2007 from www. michaelolaf. com.

peace. (n. d. ). *Dictionary. com Unabridged (v 1. 1)*. Retrieved December 01, 2007, from http:// dictionary. reference. com/browse/peace.

Polk-Lillard, P. *Montessori, A Modern Approach*. New York: Shocken Books, 1972.

Portmann, R. *The 50 Best Games for Building Self-esteem*. New York: Hinton House Publishers, 2008.

Prutzman, P., Stern, L., Burger, M. L., & Bodnhamer, G. *The Friendly Classroom for a Small Planet: A Handbook on Creative Approaches to Living and Problem Solving with Children.* New York: New Society Publishers, 1988.

Reardon, B. *Comprehensive Peace Education: Educating for Global Responsibility.* New York: Teachers College Press, 1988.

Reasoner, R. *The True Meaning of Self-esteem.* 2008. Retrieved April 7, 2008 from www. self-esteem-nase. org/whatisselfesteem. shtml.

Sapp, J. "Cooperative Learning: A Foundation for Race Dialogue." *Teaching Tolerance Magazine 30.* (2006): Retrieved April 10, 2008 from http://www. tolerance. org/teach/magazine/features. jsp?p=0&is=39&ar=684.

Seldin, T. *How to Raise an Amazing Child the Montessori Way.* New York: DK Publishing, 2006.

Schmidt , R., & Friedman, A. *Peacemaking Skills for Little Kids.* Miami FL: Grace Contrino Abrmas Peace Education Foundation, 1988.

Sher, B. *Self-esteem Games: 300 Fun Activities that Make Children Feel Good About Themselves.* New York: John Wiley & Sons, 1998.

Sherlock, M. *Living Simply with Children.* New York: Three Rivers Press, 2003.

Shure, M. (2006)."Professional Development: How Young Children Solve Problems." *Early Childhood Today 20,* (2006): 10–11.

Simpson, S. *Esteem Dreams.* [CD]. CA: Suzanne Simpson, 1999.

Standing, E. M. *Maria Montessori: Her Life and Work.* London: Hollis & Carter Limited, 1957.

Stewart, M., & Phillips, K. *Yoga for Children.* New York: Fireside Books, 1992.

University of New Hampshire Cooperative Extension. *The 3, 4 and 5-year-old child: Self esteem.* 2002. Family development fact sheet.

Vardin, P."Montessori and Gardner's Theory of Multiple Intelligences." *Montessori Life 15* (2003): 40–43.

Vestal, A., & Jones, N."Peace Building and Conflict Resolution in Preschool Children." *Journal of Research in Childhood Education 19,* (2004): 131–142.

Walsiki, A., & Carlson, L. "Group Work with Preschool Children: Effect on Emotional Awareness and Behavior." *The Journal for Specialists in Group Work 33:1* (2008): 3–21.

Walker, L. "Violence Prevention through Cooperative Learning." *Reclaiming Children and Youth 15* (2006): 32–36.

Wheeler, E., & Stomfay-Stitz, A. "Language of Peace in the Peaceful Classroom." *Childhood Education 82*, (2006): 292–293.

Wood, S. *Sensational Meditation for Children.* Asheville, NC: Satya Method Resource Center, 2006.